T0271237

Conversations with Joanna Scott

Literary Conversations Series
Monika Gehlawat
General Editor

Books by Joanna Scott

Fading, My Parmacheene Belle (New York: Ticknor & Fields, 1987; London: Bodley Head, 1988)

The Closest Possible Union (New York: Ticknor & Fields, 1988; London: Bodley Head, 1989)

Arrogance (New York: Linden Press, Simon & Schuster, 1990; London: Scribner, 1991)

Various Antidotes (New York: Henry Holt & Company, 1994)

The Manikin (New York: Henry Holt & Company, 1996)

Make Believe (Boston, New York, and London: Little, Brown and Company, 2000; London: Harvill Press, 2000)

Tourmaline (Boston, New York, and London: Little, Brown and Company, 2002)

Liberation (Boston, New York, and London: Little, Brown and Company, 2005)

Everybody Loves Somebody (New York, Boston, and London: Back Bay Books, 2006)

Follow Me (New York, Boston, and London: Back Bay Books, 2009)

De Potter's Grand Tour (New York: Farrar, Straus and Giroux, 2014)

Careers for Women (New York, Boston, and London: Little, Brown and Company, 2017)

Excuse Me While I Disappear (New York, Boston, and London: Little, Brown and Company, forthcoming 2021)

Conversations with Joanna Scott

Edited by Michael Lackey

University Press of Mississippi / Jackson

The University Press of Mississippi is the scholarly publishing agency of
the Mississippi Institutions of Higher Learning: Alcorn State University,
Delta State University, Jackson State University, Mississippi State University,
Mississippi University for Women, Mississippi Valley State University,
University of Mississippi, and University of Southern Mississippi.

www.upress.state.ms.us

The University Press of Mississippi is a member
of the Association of University Presses.

First printing 2020
∞

Library of Congress Cataloging-in-Publication Data

Names: Scott, Joanna, 1960– interviewee, interviewer. | Lackey, Michael,
    editor.
Title: Conversations with Joanna Scott / edited by Michael Lackey.
Other titles: Literary conversations series.
Description: Jackson : University Press of Mississippi, 2020. | Series:
    Literary conversations series | Includes index.
Identifiers: LCCN 2020010585 (print) | LCCN 2020010586 (ebook) | ISBN
    9781496829320 (hardback) | ISBN 9781496829337 (trade paperback) | ISBN
    9781496829344 (epub) | ISBN 9781496829351 (epub) | ISBN 9781496829368
    (pdf) | ISBN 9781496829375 (pdf)
Subjects: LCSH: Scott, Joanna, 1960-—Interviews. | Authors, American—20th
    century—Interviews. | BISAC: BIOGRAPHY & AUTOBIOGRAPHY / Literary
    Figures
Classification: LCC PS3569.C636 Z46 2020 (print) | LCC PS3569.C636
    (ebook) | DDC 813/.6—dc23
LC record available at https://lccn.loc.gov/2020010585
LC ebook record available at https://lccn.loc.gov/2020010586

British Library Cataloging-in-Publication Data available

Contents

Introduction

Recipient of the MacArthur Fellowship, often referred to as the "genius grant," Joanna Scott has been recognized as one of America's most prominent writers since the 1980s. Given the high quality of her work, she has been honored with prestigious awards and fellowships, including a Guggenheim Fellowship in 1988, the Rosenthal Family Foundation Award for Literature in 1991, a Lannan Literary Award for Fiction in 1999, a fellowship from the Santa Maddalena Foundation in 2007, an honorary degree as Doctor of Letters from Trinity College in Hartford in 2009, a Lannan Foundation Residency in spring 2015, and a Bogliasco Fellowship in spring 2017.

Born on June 22, 1960, to Walter Lee and Yvonne, Scott grew up in Darien, Connecticut. By her own account, "the freedom" she "had as a kid was extraordinary." In her interview with Bradford Morrow, she describes her three older brothers (Matthew, Marco, and Peter) and herself as "half wild" children. From an early age, she "could go [wherever] and do whatever" she "pleased," and that liberty nourished within her "a connection to the world and the illusion of escape." But "as the youngest sibling—and only daughter," she felt alone, which led her to start "secretly writing to fight the isolation." This was a startling development, and indicative of Scott's intellectual independence, because, as she claims in an interview for the Writers Forum with poet Ralph Black and novelist Anne Panning, she did not come from a bookish family. To the contrary, she says that her family was "big on football." At around this same time, she became enamored of the "paradoxical pleasure" of books. Writers and works that influenced her during this period include "Tolkien, Burnett, Lewis Carroll, [and] Harper Lee," as well as "old English tales, the *World Book Encyclopedia*, and a musty copy of the Bible—New Revised Standard Version" (Morrow). It was William Faulkner, however, who had a decisive impact. As a high school student, Scott found a 1946 Modern Library edition of Faulkner's *The Sound and the Fury* and *As I Lay Dying* at a local yard sale, and she remembers "how fascinated and disoriented" she felt as she "turned the pages, reading through the opening chapter of *The Sound and the Fury* in a sweat prompted less by the heat than by the weird, unsettling resonance of Faulkner's language." It was at this point that Scott "started writing what" she "dared to call fiction in response to Faulkner" (Morrow).

She graduated from Darien High School in 1978 and then enrolled at Trinity College in Connecticut, where she "studied English literature with fiction writers Stephen Minot and Thalia Selz, both of whom encouraged her writing," as she tells Daniel Nester. After spending one semester in Rome and one year at Barnard College, Scott graduated with honors in English from Trinity in 1983. But instead of going directly to graduate school, she became "an assistant to Geri Thoma at the Elaine Markson Literary Agency [in New York City] and received an informal education in the inner workings of the publishing industry." This experience gave her insight into the professional world, but it also established an important connection, as Thoma "would eventually serve as Scott's agent for her first novel" and continues to represent her. One year later, she enrolled in "Brown University's graduate writing program, where she worked with such luminaries as Susan Sontag, Robert Coover, and John Hawkes, with whom she had a mentorship" (Nester).

Having completed her MA in 1985, Scott stayed at Brown for another year to teach undergraduates. In 1987, she secured her first tenure-track job at the University of Maryland, and the following year, she accepted a tenure-track post at the University of Rochester, where she continues to teach and where she was named Roswell Smith Burrows Professor in 1999. She is married to James Longenbach, a notable poet and literary critic. His books include *Fleet River*, *The Iron Key*, *The Resistance to Poetry*, and *The Art of the Poetic Line*. They have two daughters.

Startling about Scott is her ability to excel in so many genres. American novelist and founding editor of the journal *Conjunctions*, Morrow praises Scott's 1996 novel *The Manikin*, a finalist for the Pulitzer Prize for Fiction. Specifically, Morrow admires the "Gothic sensibility" in the work, which is why he compares her to writers like Edgar Allan Poe and Charlotte Brontë. Maureen Howard won the National Book Critics Circle Award, and she praises Scott's use of the ballad form in her 2009 novel *Follow Me*. American novelist Bruce Bauman marvels at Scott's ability to write "philosophical and politically inspired works," which is why he compares her to Iris Murdoch. Scott's extraordinary range explains why English novelist Nick Hornby says in a *New York Times* review that "Joanna Scott is a Michael Jordan: she has talent to burn" and the poet Nester refers to her in his interview as a "writer's writer."

Perhaps Scott's most important contribution has been to the literary world of biofiction. Different from both biography and historical fiction, biofiction is literature that names its protagonist after an actual historical figure, and Scott has significantly advanced studies of the aesthetic form as both a practitioner and critic. The first example in her oeuvre is *Arrogance*, a biographical novel about the Austrian artist Egon Schiele. Published in 1990, this novel foregrounds Schiele's upbringing as a son of an abusive father, his near-incestuous relationship with his sister, his desire and drive to become an artist, his shifting relationship with and allegiance to Gustav Klimt, and his trial and imprisonment for pornography. Critically acclaimed when first released (it was a finalist for the PEN/Faulkner Award), this work continues to receive attention and to enhance Scott's reputation. The timing of the publication of this novel in part accounts for its contemporary relevance, for it was in the 1990s that the biographical novel started to become a dominant literary form. J. M. Coetzee, Margaret Atwood, Michael Cunningham, Charles Johnson, and Russell Banks are just a few celebrated writers who published stellar biographical novels during the decade. But Scott innovated with this literary form before all of them, and she has also done much to answer some questions that have perplexed scholars. For instance, many scholars treat the biographical novel as a form of biography, which means that fidelity to the biographical record is one of the primary criteria for determining a work's effectiveness and quality. But in her 2016 essay "On Hoaxes, Humbugs, and Fictional Portraiture," Scott set the scholarly record straight about the biographical novelist's usage (not representation) of the biographical subject by claiming: "I was not pretending that my Schiele was the real Schiele. I just wanted him to be real" (103). The aesthetic objective of the biographical novelist is not to accurately represent the biographical subject. It is to fictionalize the life of the historical figure in order to project into being the author's own aesthetic vision.

This is exactly what Scott did in many of the short biofictional stories (about Francis Huber, Madame Coutelier de Bretteville, and Dorothea Dix) from her 1994 collection, *Various Antidotes*. Nominated for a PEN/Faulkner Award, this book won the *Southern Review*'s Short Fiction Prize and was named among twenty-five best books of the year by the *Voice Literary Supplement*. Moreover, the collection includes two award-winning stories: "A Borderline Case" won the Aga Khan Award for the best story published in the *Paris Review* in 1992, and the story "Convicta et Combusta" won the Pushcart Prize, which "honors the best 'poetry, short fiction, essays or literary whatnot' published in the small presses over the previous year." The collection's opening story, "Concerning Mold Upon the Skin, Etc.," which was included in the 1993 anthology of *Best American Short Stories*, is vintage biofiction. The protagonist is Antonie van Leeuwenhoek, a Dutch scientist and businessman who is considered today one of the founding fathers of microbiology. Driven by an obsession that alienates and even destroys his family to some degree, Leeuwenhoek is overjoyed when he realizes the potential impact of his discoveries with his microscope: "This was the lasting consequence of his invention: he had forever changed the nature of belief. Nothing visible to the naked eye could be trusted anymore, for everything had a secret microscopic life. He, the master of magnification, had made visible the unimaginable" (11). On the surface, this story is about Leeuwenhoek. But if we understand the uncanny power and the ambiguous semiotics of biofiction, these lines tell us as much about Scott's ideas about art as they do about the Dutch inventor. In essence, the story uses Leeuwenhoek not to get to his consciousness but to clarify what the artist does. Accordingly, what Leeuwenhoek did in the world of science, Scott does in the world of fiction. As one of the narrators from *Arrogance* says, "it is the artist's responsibility to educate" the "eyes" (68) of the audience, and for Scott, this means that the fiction writer's ability to expose the "secret microscopic life" of consciousness would lead people to distrust what is "visible to the naked eye," an act of literary "magnification" that makes "visible the unimaginable." Put more succinctly, surface projections belie the more complex and shadowy realities of human interiors. Such is the stuff that Scott's fiction is made of.

Readers get much more insight into Scott's view of biofiction through her 2014 novel *De Potter's Grand Tour*, which is about her great-grandfather, Armand de Potter. This work was the Editor's Choice of the *New York Times Book Review* and a *Chicago Tribune* Best Book of the Year. In the novel, de Potter leads world tours and glories in his collection of ancient Egyptian art. But there are problems. To establish a reputable and successful tourist agency, de Potter deceives everyone, including his wife, into believing that he is much more than he really is. In essence, de Potter plays a big hoax on everyone. But ultimately, the hoax is on him, because he eventually discovers that some of his ancient Egyptian antiquities, for which he paid a fortune and went into considerable debt, are forgeries.

When Scott was working on *De Potter's Grand Tour*, she did an interview with me titled "The Masking Art of the Biographical Novel." While that interview focuses mainly on *Arrogance*, what she says in it clearly relates to *De Potter's Grand Tour*. At the time, Scott was "thinking about the artificial nature of fiction," and to define it, she realized the value of "the metaphor of the mask." As a novelist, Scott claims, "I'm probably closer in spirit to a masked performer wandering through the fog of Venice during Carnivale than to a historian." Notice how Scott distances herself from history. The scholarly tendency has been to define the biographical novel as a subgenre of the historical novel, but Scott indicates why this is a mistake. For the author of a biographical novel, the emphasis is not on the actual "historical figure." Rather, it is on the artist's vision as expressed through "the dynamic relationship between the mask wearer [novelist] and the mask [fictionalized figure] itself," which is why Scott concludes that "it is the ingenuity of the performance rather than the precision of the resemblance that counts." Therefore, instead of asking whether biographical novelists accurately represent the biographical subject or his/her time period, readers should be asking how authors use the historical figure (the way "the mask is put into action") in order to project something new into being. As Scott says: "The deeper I got into writing *Arrogance*, the more my attention went to creating something new rather than repeating what was already known."

The same principle applies to *De Potter's Grand Tour*. In a crucial moment in his life, de Potter shares his philosophy of art with others. The great artist is not the one that persuades "us that the false thing is real" but rather convinces "us to forget reality altogether" (182). This is the case because reality is not a pre-existent Platonic Form waiting to be discovered. It is a provisional conceptual formation that "some influential artist has given us" (183). Is this an accurate representation of de Potter's philosophy of art? In other words, did he really make such claims? Given Scott's aesthetic approach, which is to take de Potter "out of history, out of the factual swamp, and to reinvent him as a fictional character" (Lackey, "Masking"), these are misguided questions. Here are some more suitable questions: How did Scott fictionalize and alter de Potter's life in order to express her view of the artistic construction of conceptual reality? How does she use de Potter's life to illuminate the negotiation between an individual's projected sense of reality and the projected realities external to self? In short, *Arrogance* and *De Potter's Grand Tour* are not biographical works about Schiele and de Potter. They are novels that fictionalize Schiele and de Potter to express Scott's view of life and the world.

The most recent novel, *Careers for Women* (2017), gives us new and deeper insight into Scott's craft as well as the biographical novel more generally. The novel tells the story of the fictional character Pauline Moreau, whose life is determined in large measure by two business executives. The fictional Robert Whittaker Jr. works for Alumacore, a company that puts profits above people and poisons the environment through illegal dumping and emissions. Whittaker, who is married, impregnates the seventeen-year-old Pauline and gives her hush money to relocate. After working some odd jobs in New York City and descending into poverty and then prostitution, Pauline meets the novel's other main character, Lee K. Jaffe, an actual person who served from 1944 through 1965 as director of public relations at the Port Authority in New York City. Jaffe hires Pauline, giving her the opportunity to salvage a happy and meaningful life for herself and her daughter, but Whittaker's toxic lifestyle eventually leads to Pauline's death.

What makes *Careers for Women* so important is the degree to which it reveals Scott's aesthetic objectives. In 1937 Georg Lukács published *The Historical Novel*, which treats the biographical novel as a subgenre or version of the historical novel. But many contemporary biographical novelists, such as Colum McCann, Colm Tóibín, Olga Tokarczuk, and Rosa Montero, express reservations about the historical novel and insist that they do not write historical fiction. In a recent public forum, Scott locates herself within the biofiction literary tradition by saying that she is "not alone in sharing some deep skepticism in terms of what we used to call the historical novel" ("Roundtable"). The logical product of the Enlightenment's valorization of science and reason, history was increasingly treated as a hard science during the nineteenth century, which resulted in the historical novel's privileging of the way environmental conditions and historical forces shape and determine human subjectivity, an aesthetic act that subordinates at best and eliminates at worst human autonomy and individual agency. To counter the historical novel, there was a shift in emphasis from history to biography, from scientific determinism to individual autonomy. While Scott deeply respects science and history, she has a deeper commitment to human mystery and individual autonomy, and this in part explains her reservations about historical fiction and her propensity to author biofiction.

It is important to note that for Scott we do not have to choose between science and literature, facts and the imagination. At stake for her is the intrusion of science or history-as-science into the world of art. Scientists should do science, and historians should do history, and Scott respects and values both as such. But neither should demand that artists subordinate the literary to the scientific or the historical, because literature is and does its own thing, which is oftentimes in irreconcilable conflict with what science and history do. This explains why Scott resists the contemporary impulse to turn to the empirical to legitimize fiction: "Imagination does not need to be made legitimate. The creative work that the mind does when it is leaving behind verifiable information won't be saved and made newly legitimate if it is imbued with facts" ("Roundtable"). As a devout Enlightenment rationalist, Lukács formulates a science-based approach to history and then demands that novelists incorporate that approach into their aesthetic. But for Scott, while she frequently uses science and history in her fiction, the fiction is of primary and ultimate importance, and thus cannot be subordinate to either science or history.

Biofiction's focus on autonomy explains why Scott is drawn to the life of Jaffe. Jaffe is not a predictable figure, thus making her unsuitable in a historical novel. Lukács stipulates that one of the first and most important aesthetic laws is that the protagonist of the historical novel be an invented figure, which differentiates it from the biographical novel. This is not just an idiosyncratic recommendation on Lukács's part. It is the logical consequence of his scientific approach to history and his Marxist view of the novel. The protagonist must function as a representative symbol of the people, the nation, and the age, a figure that embodies "social trends and historical forces" (34). Symbolic not just of an average person, this figure represents the whole nation and age. This explains why Lukács believes that "the central figure" of the work should be a "mediocre, prosaic hero" (34). To give the character too much personality, individuality, or autonomy would undermine the protagonist's function to symbolize a larger representative reality from the past. As Lukács says of Walter Scott, whom he considers the ideal historical novelist: "he never creates eccentric figures, figures who fall psychologically outside the atmosphere of his age" (60).

Scott's Jaffe is the antithesis of the representative protagonist found in the historical novel. Quirky and unpredictable, she is a visionary figure who defies convention, which is why she is the ideal subject of a biographical novel. In a public forum about *Careers for Women*, Scott emphasizes that it was Jaffe's outsider way of being that caught her attention. She discovered Jaffe in a newspaper article about the destruction of the World Trade Center. Here is how Scott describes the work: The article "begins by saying: 'You would not expect the head of publicity for the Port Authority to be a slim woman wearing a beret.' That's true" ("Roundtable"). With its focus on the unique, the original, and the autonomous, the biographical novel is less interested in giving readers representative characters from the past than in using quirky and original figures to model the process of living an autonomous life and thereby to inspire readers to become active creators of a new reality for the future.

Thus, it makes sense that Jaffe "creates a kind of center for the novel," as Scott claims in the roundtable, for she is a figure that embodies "strength and vision" (Bauman). Scott specifies the kind of effect she hopes a character like Jaffe would have on her audience: "I want to absorb readers, but I want them to come away with a sense of heightened possibility, of imagination that's perhaps lit up a little bit more, a sense of their own creative powers" (Tschernkowitsch). Lukács (and historical novelists more generally) thinks that the author should create a fictive protagonist that functions as a symbol to accurately represent the past as it really was, an aesthetic feat that would help clarify for us in the present how we have come to be as we currently are, while Scott (and biographical novelists more generally) thinks that authors should use figures from the past in order to model the process of human autonomy, thus empowering readers in the present to activate their imagination in order to create new ways of thinking and being for the future. For Scott, literature has an uncanny power to enable people to engage and experience the world in new, fresh, and meaningful ways. As she says in her 2015 interview with American novelist Martin Naparsteck: "I have always appreciated the power of fiction to make us responsive, not just to get us absorbed imaginatively, but then to give us the ability to go out and see the world with a freshness and intensity."

That Scott would reject a Lukács-inspired aesthetic form and turn to something like biofiction makes perfect sense given her intellectual and aesthetic commitments. The nineteenth century witnessed the rise of positivism, a deterministic system of thought that defined everything according to the strict and mechanistic laws of cause and effect. Literature, science, philosophy, psychology, history, economics, and politics were just a few fields of intellectual inquiry that were heavily impacted. But artists and thinkers like Edouard Manet, Arthur Rimbaud, Friedrich Nietzsche, and Oscar Wilde, to mention only a notable few, committed themselves to the intellectual and aesthetic project of safeguarding human interiors, that part of the individual that endlessly creates meaning and sense. Scott fits comfortably within this latter intellectual tradition. Indeed, Scott is very clear in distancing herself from the Lukács literary tradition in her interview with me. After noting that "Lukács was reacting against" "the modernist immersion in individual subjectivity," Scott says that she "was nurtured by that immersion and it is absolutely what I love. I came to be a writer because I was reading Woolf and Faulkner and Conrad, all good distorters who remind us of the value of individual existence" (Lackey, "Masking").

In her 1998 interview with Howard, Scott, discussing Howard's work, reveals how literature functions to illuminate the human inner life: "I feel in your work and especially in this new novel [*A Lover's Almanac*] that I am very much seeing myself holding the book. There's an intense self-consciousness that makes me think about where I am in my life." Readers may be reading about historical or fictional figures, but great literature enables them to see something inside themselves that had previously been hidden. This is not always a pleasant experience, for sometimes people are in thrall to sick or twisted systems of thought. For instance, in *Careers for Women*, Scott uses the character of Whittaker "to trace how violence can result from a slow-burning corruption, a way of thinking that involves weird, contorted logic" (Bauman). In a sense, Scott sees the literary author as a cultural diagnostician, as someone who can "keep the [cultural] problems visible" (Morrow). Understanding the near-implacable logic and compulsion of systems of thought, what Scott refers to as "that tug of inevitability" (Naparsteck 2015), explains her appreciation and usage of psychology. As she says in her interview with Panning and Black: "There is definitely room to be skeptical of the simplistic cause-and-effect psychology that diminishes the intricacy of behavior. But we can't give up on psychology."

Scott is committed to exposing and defining specific psychologies, no matter how contorted or perverse, which is why she values so highly the study of psychology and the usage of it in literature. But what matters most to her is that uncanny ability to evade psychological determinism and to originate a new way of thinking and being. As she says in her 2010 interview with Howard: we "need literature to keep teaching us how meaning can be made." For Scott, novelists do not use established systems of knowledge in order to illuminate what Lukács refers to as "objective reality." To the contrary, novelists picture how systems of knowledge are produced. The emphasis here is on the autonomous creation rather than the mechanical usage of knowledge. As Scott claims, "the fundamental joy" in literature "is in the act of invention" (Lackey, "Masking"). And what she does in literature is what she hopes to impart to her reader. In short, Scott is obsessed with the originating power and creative potential of the mind: "To watch the artist in action, working on or responding to something—I learn from that, I learn about what we can do and what we can think and what we haven't thought before. Every new sentence teaches me something new about the potential of the mind" (Lackey, "Masking").

Over the last ten years there has been a growing sense of urgency in Scott's writing, which, in part, explains a key development in her career. In 2008 she took on the role of public intellectual by becoming a regular contributor to *The Nation*, America's oldest continuously published magazine. Seemingly just book reviews, her articles are valuable for many reasons:

Scott locates the work of groundbreaking and difficult artists within specific intellectual traditions, writes in a way that is accessible to a general audience, offers excellent insight into individual works, and discloses much that is meaningful to her as a critic and writer. Her first article, "Where Now? Let's Go!," brilliantly analyzes specific passages from Donald Barthelme's works in order to clarify how his fiction explores "the dimensions of the absurd—the shared cosmic joke of life and the pathos of grappling with it" (32), a literary approach that puts Barthelme in the company of James Joyce, Gertrude Stein, Samuel Beckett, and Thomas Pynchon.

Her second article, "Telling It Slant," focuses on Isak Dinesen, whose work urges "us to recognize the reality of the artificial," because "truth in stories" is to be found "not just in sincere confessions but in the deliberate lies and imagined possibilities, the magic and fantasy and all the other unreal elements that go into the concoction of identity" (28). This is a wonderful insight about Dinesen, but what makes this article so valuable is the way Scott uses the marginalization of Dinesen to diagnose a particular cultural ailment. The explosion of confession through "the democratic exposures of the web" leaves little "room for imagination except to demand its allegiance to the person, which may leave readers less inclined to find value in the extravagant lies of fiction" (25). Fiction gives readers something of major significance, and given some recent cultural developments, like the confessional mode frequently found on the web, the turn away from literature can have devastating consequences on our ability to understand and construct our identities.

In 2012, Scott published "Till the Knowing Ends," a review of William Gass's *Life Sentences: Literary Judgments and Accounts.* As a writer who published fourteen books, including five novels, Gass demands that readers learn to imagine "living other lives" (27). Such an act will not lead to comforting truths or an intellectual redemption, for as Gass and Scott conclude, "Nothing has been righted here" (24). And yet, "we are renewed through art," Scott claims, "in particular, through the art of writing as Gass enacts it" (30). Lest you think this is a facile consolation, Scott concludes with Gass's very distinct and productive form of rage: "When we put ourselves in his place, we notice that his rage is for the world, not against it" (30).

The 2015 article "Liberating Reading," which should be required reading for undergraduates in the humanities, addresses a topic dear to Scott's heart and central to her aesthetic. What is the value of reading challenging, extremely difficult fiction? And how can we make the case for such reading in an age that privileges profits and instant gratification? Toni Morrison notes that "fiction gives us knowledge" (27), Virginia Woolf argues that it refines our perceptions, and James Wood claims that it awakens "us from the deadening 'sleep of our attention'" and enables us "to look more closely at our world" (30). All of these writers understand how difficult reading can create the intellectual conditions for a more probing and accurate engagement with the world and lead to more "independence and empowerment" (31). But in this article, Scott borders on despair. As a fan of difficult modernist literature, she has championed throughout her career the works of Faulkner and Joyce. But given the growing power of predatory capitalism and the digital humanities, Scott seems to be having a change of heart and mind: "I am among the readers who thought modernism, along with other richly challenging literary periods, had staying power. Now I'm not so sure" (31). This is a different Scott than the one who authored *Arrogance* and *The Manikin*.

Other articles focus on Coetzee's artistic method of telling seemingly autobiographical truth slant, street photographer Vivian Maier's uncanny ability "to find the perfect angle of vision" in order "to create extraordinary images out of ordinary scenes" ("Self-Portrait" 27), Faulkner's precarious engagement with language in order to control an "unorderly, unwieldy life" ("Ragged" 24), and Georges Perec's gift to readers of "a refreshingly flexible model for narrative" with "inconclusive endings" ("Never" 30). Scott's articles in *The Nation* contain compact but profound reflections about epistemology, culture, literature, and the mind. They are valuable not just because Scott is so intelligent and well-read, but because they give us insight into who we are and hint at what we can become.

There is a reason why Scott's work has inspired so many and had such an impact for now more than thirty years. Her dazzling prose captivates readers, her daring imagination challenges well-established conventions, and her aesthetic precision and control illuminate unexpected realities. One would think that such gifts could only be found in writing that has been heavily revised multiple times. But as readers of the enclosed interviews will discover, all of these exceptional traits are part of Scott's everyday way of being.

ML

Bibliography

Hornby, Nick. Review of *Make Believe*. *New York Times*, February 20, 2000, http://movies2.nytimes.com/books/00/02/20/reviews/000220.20hornbyt.html.

Lukács, Georg. *The Historical Novel*. Lincoln: University of Nebraska Press, 1983.

Scott, Joanna. *Arrogance*. New York: Picador, 1990.

Scott, Joanna. "Concerning Mold Upon the Skin, Etc." In *Various Antidotes*, 1–11. New York: Henry Holt and Company, 1994.

Scott, Joanna. *De Potter's Grand Tour*. New York: Farrar, Straus and Giroux, 2014.

Scott, Joanna. "In the Theater of Isak Dinesen." *The Nation* 289, no. 6 (August 31, 2009): 25–28.

Scott, Joanna. "Liberating Reading." *The Nation* 301, no. 7/8 (August 17, 2015): 27–31.

Scott, Joanna. "Never-Endings." *The Nation* 303, no. 9/10 (August 29, 2016): 27–31.

Scott, Joanna. "On Hoaxes, Humbugs, and Fictional Portraiture." In *Biographical Fiction: A Reader*, edited by Michael Lackey, 98–103. New York and London: Bloomsbury, 2017.

Scott, Joanna. "Ragged, Unkempt, Strange." *The Nation* 295, no. 24 (December 10, 2012): 17–24.

Scott, Joanna. "Self-Portrait in a Sheet Mirror." *The Nation* 294, no. 24 (June 11, 2012): 27–32.

Scott, Joanna. "Telling It Slant." *The Nation* 290, no. 6 (February 15, 2010): 25–29.

Scott, Joanna. "Till the Knowing Ends." *The Nation* 294, no. 13 (March 26, 2012): 27–30.

Scott, Joanna. "Where Now? Let's Go!" *The Nation* 286, no. 16 (April 28, 2008): 31–36.

Chronology

by the *Los Angeles Times* and the *New York Times* and a finalist for the *Los Angeles Times* Book Award.

2005 Publishes *Liberation*, which wins the Ambassador Book Award from the English Speaking Union.

2006 Publishes her collection of stories *Everybody Loves Somebody* and wins the Smart Family Foundation Award from the *Yale Review* for the short story "The Queen of Sheba Is Afraid of Snow."

2008 Becomes a contributor to *The Nation*.

2009 Publishes her novel *Follow Me*, which is named a *New York Times* Notable Book.

2014 Publishes her novel *De Potter's Grand Tour* and the short story "The Knowledge Gallery." This story, originally published in *Conjunctions* in 2014, is reprinted in *The Pushcart Prize Anthology* in 2015 and reprinted by the New York Public Library subway project.

2017 Publishes her novel *Careers for Women*.

Conversations with Joanna Scott

Joanna Scott

Paul Perilli / 1996

From *Poets & Writers* 24, no. 3 (January/February 1996): 61–67. Reprinted by permission of the publisher, Poets & Writers, Inc., 90 Broad Street, Suite 2100, New York, NY 10004. www.pw.org.

"Yet, it is the nourishment that wonder seeks, life," states the narrator in Joanna Scott's short story "Concerning Mold Upon the Skin, Etc." which opens her collection *Various Antidotes* (Henry Holt, 1994) and was included in *Best American Short Stories 1993* (Houghton Mifflin). While this statement is the narrator's reaction to the initial microscopic study of a drop of water by the seventeenth-century Dutchman Anton von Leeuwenhoek, it also can be used to exemplify the sense of wonder that Scott creates through her own work and the wide range of subjects and characters that sustain her fiction.

"History and information are sources of inspiration for me," Scott answers when asked where she finds the ideas on which she has based her four books, which include three novels. "They provoke me to imagine, to create stories around actual facts. I love the great encyclopedic novels like Melville's *Moby Dick* and *Life: A User's Manual* by Georges Perec. The way information is related in them through narrative is exciting and illuminating."

"Concerning Mold Upon the Skin, Etc." is representative of the kind of challenging projects that Scott has developed using a precise historical context and language. While researching eccentric topics from the history of medicine, which is the loosely organizing subject of *Various Antidotes*, Scott was attracted to the outsider status of Leeuwenhoek's character and career.

"I liked writing about someone who wasn't involved in the scientific vocabulary of the day," Scott says. "It was interesting for me to try to explore the mind of someone who was working in intense isolation. And the metaphor of the microscope seemed rich."

The stories in *Various Antidotes*, which was a finalist for the 1995 PEN/Faulkner Foundation Award, are more than fictionalized accounts of those who made medical discoveries and advanced medical practices. They also include one or more characters who indirectly made a contribution to medical science. In "Concerning Mold Upon the Skin, Etc." Leeuwenhoek's daughter Marie also plays an important role. It is her dutiful, nurturing service that enables him to devote the time he needs to undertake his work, and their relationship is the story's central focus. Indeed, Leeuwenhoek's name is never used in the story as if to insist on both the importance of Marie's character and the fictive nature of his own. "I purposely forced characters who are not included in the history into these situations," Scott says. "I felt they belonged to me. They were my inventions."

Joanna Scott's creative inventions began to take shape when as a child she composed stories about the tiny clay characters that populated her dioramas. She grew up in Darien, Connecticut, where she was born in 1960 and attended public school. Her father worked in advertising, and her mother was a psychologist for the schools in nearby Stamford. Her brother Marco is a musician, Matt is the director of an independent television station, and Peter is an anesthesiologist.

"Having three older brothers made me feel like an outsider," Scott says. "As the youngest child and only girl I was not included in much that went on among them, and this forced me to try to make my isolation exciting."

As an undergraduate, Scott attended Trinity College in Hartford. She majored in English literature and studied creative writing with fiction writers Stephen Minot and Thalia Selz and poet Hugh Ogden. "They encouraged the inherent idiosyncrasies of my fiction, and this gave me the support and confidence to continue with it," Scott says. During this time she spent one semester in Rome studying Renaissance literature and Italian film. She also enrolled in Barnard for a year as a visiting student. While there she helped to edit its literary magazine and took a semester off to work as a copy editor on the "Miss Manners" newspaper column and on comic strips and crossword puzzles for United Features Syndicate.

After graduating in 1983, Scott moved to New York City. Having spent many moments in Darien listening to the nearby commuter trains, cars, and trucks speed by on their way into the city, she felt this was the only possible direction for her to go. "Those sounds were important to me," she says. "Growing up outside of New York I thought everyone eventually moved there. I worked in the bakery across from the train station where I watched the commuters go into the city in the morning and always wanted to follow them in."

Scott went to New York knowing that she wanted to write fiction and once there attempted to find related employment to support it. "I went to a career counselor at Trinity and was told I should be either a librarian or an advertising copywriter." She spent a year working for the Elaine Markson Literary Agency, a job she found from a posting on a bulletin board in the Barnard employment office. "I was the assistant to Geri Thoma," Scott says. "I answered the phone and read unsolicited manuscripts. But my favorite thing to do was to read the correspondence with authors and writers. It gave me an idea as to what really happens in publishing, how a manuscript turns into a book. I saw publishing as something that was possible rather than the magical transformation I'd previously thought it was." She shared an apartment with friends on West 111th Street. After work and on the weekends she wrote "many failed short stories" that she permanently filed away instead of mailing to journals and magazines.

Scott left New York to attend Brown University, where she received an MA in 1985. She studied mostly with John Hawkes and Robert Coover and also took a class with Susan Sontag, who was a visiting writer during Scott's first semester. The three semesters of workshops were a valuable experience for her. "I never received such harsh criticism," Scott says. "It prepared me for tough book reviews." The comments she received from Coover and Hawkes were insightful, forceful, and convincing. Coover wrote on student stories with colored pens, and Scott says it was sometimes difficult to locate an area that wasn't highlighted. Hawkes used a manual typewriter to write two or three small sheets of comments per story. "There was a humorous edge to his criticism and sometimes I'd laugh my way through it," she says. "Sometimes, of course, I'd moan in despair."

While she was a student at Brown, Scott had a part-time job working in the rare books library. She was responsible for noting information about nineteenth-century books of poetry that would be entered on a new computerized catalogue system. "I was able to sit for hours and read these books," she says. "I was fascinated by the prefatory apologies the authors wrote to their readers back then. I also learned something about the nineteenth century and the fate of obscure writers."

An important turning point for Scott came during her final semester. "The story I wrote for my last workshop was told in the voice of an old fisherman and was different from much of the other fiction I'd been writing at the time, where I set my young narrators out in search of an identity, had them ask a lot of big questions about the meaning of life," she says. Her workshop teacher Hawkes encouraged her to write another story using the archaic Pennsylvania Dutch voice of the old fisherman. Scott accepted his challenge and wrote a one-act play, which eventually became the second chapter of her first novel. Feeling she had something lengthy to explore she continued to write chapters. "I loved the feeling of having this narrative go on and on," Scott says. "It was liberating to have created a character completely different from me. Before this my writing had been tentative. I didn't know how to use my imagination properly. I'd write straightforward sentences without a lot of embellishment or metaphor. And the metaphors I did write did not feel spontaneous. I'd reach outside the story for them instead of having them come from within the narrator or subject."

After graduating, Scott stayed on at Brown to teach creative writing to undergraduates. During that year she finished a draft of her novel and sent the completed manuscript to Thoma at the Elaine Markson Literary Agency. Thoma agreed to represent it and *Fading, My Parmacheene Belle* (Ticknor & Fields, 1987) soon became her first published novel. Having the book accepted transformed Scott's image of herself as a writer. During the next year she lived off the small advance she received; this showed her that writing was a profession that might support her.

The idea for Scott's second novel, *The Closest Possible Union* (Ticknor & Fields, 1988), developed after she was browsing in a library. "I was researching a story about someone who becomes obsessed with a dead poet, wants to exhume the body that's buried in another country and bring it back to the United States. But instead I came upon a book about slaves and slave ships." The book contained letters, journals, and reports written by those who sailed the Middle Passage in the nineteenth century. Scott opened the book to a letter written by a boy who had been a captain's apprentice. In it, the boy described seeing a slave hamstrung and then thrown into the water by a sailor on the ship. Scott was struck by the childishness of the boy's tone coupled with the violence he had witnessed. She decided to make the central image of the story the blood that the boy described floating on the surface of the water "that faded to nothing." "I set out to write a short story and expected this image to appear eight pages later," Scott says. "But I didn't get there for 150 pages, and it became a novel."

A fellowship from the Guggenheim Foundation closely followed the publication of *The Closest Possible Union*, and this gave Scott time off to write and travel to Vienna to research her third novel, *Arrogance* (Simon & Schuster, 1991). *Arrogance* was nominated for the 1991 PEN/Faulkner Award and received the 1991 Richard and Hinda Rosenthal Foundation Award from the American Academy and Institute of Arts and Letters. It is a fragmented portrait of the Austrian expressionist painter Egon Schiele, who was infamous in Vienna art circles in the early part of the century for his controversial depictions of men and women. Scott tells Schiele's story from several different points of view, including that of his mistress and frequent subject Vallie and of an unnamed teenager whom Schiele suspected of being the accuser that helped send him to prison on charges of corrupting the morals of young girls. Scott also includes excerpts from Schiele's letters and diaries and several long descriptions of Vienna at the turn of the century that set the physical, historical, and psychological environment in which Schiele lived and worked. In *Arrogance*, Scott does not follow Schiele's twenty-eight years in chronological order but instead shifts back and forth between different periods and events of his life, from scenes of his childhood to his twenty-eight-day imprisonment to conversations he had with his teacher and rival Gustav Klimt. The overall effect is a fictional montage that creates a vivid impression of the artist and those around him.

"I went to a show on Viennese art in 1988 at the Museum of Modern Art in New York," Scott says. "Schiele had some drawings in one of the smaller galleries. I saw a group of people staring and laughing at a self-portrait of him standing naked, and that's when I became fascinated with his work." In the following weeks, Scott began reading about Schiele's life and envisioning fictional possibilities. "It was the audience's disgust at his work that finally attracted me to him. I started out writing about the arrogance of the Viennese audience who judged his work, but later I saw his bravado and arrogance, and the book is about this too."

"Teaching and writing go together for me," Scott says. "I find them complementary. When I thought of making a career as a writer I included teaching. I like working with my students, and find I learn from them. It also gives me the opportunity to read with a careful critical eye. I can be a lazy reader otherwise."

Besides teaching at Brown, Scott has taught at the University of Maryland and, since 1988, at the University of Rochester, where she is a professor of English. Her husband James Longenbach, who has published his own poetry as well as three critical books on modern poetry, teaches poetry and Shakespeare in the same department. Scott teaches fiction workshops to undergraduate and graduate students and classes on the contemporary novel and on the novels of Charles Dickens.

Since 1992 Scott has had the good fortune to be able to take off several semesters to concentrate solely on her writing. In May of that year a phone call interrupted a few hours of time she had set aside to spend with her then nine-month-old daughter Kathryn. The male voice at the other end of the line informed her she had received a fellowship from the John D. and Catherine T. MacArthur Foundation. Scott laughs when she recalls her initial reaction doubting the caller's veracity, and then stunned disbelief after she phoned the Chicago foundation back and was told again that she had in fact received a fellowship.

"It was a great relief to get it," Scott says. "About that time I'd been feeling that with teaching and raising my daughter I might not have enough time to write."

She is using some of her MacArthur fellowship to take the 1995–96 academic year off to work on new short fiction.

Scott is not entirely comfortable writing about subjects on which she is less than an expert. She still expects those having more knowledge and experience in art or medicine to call her fictional bluff but so far has received little criticism on this matter. Nevertheless, it is a worry she has regarding her recently published novel *The Manikin* (Henry Holt, 1996), which is set in an isolated country estate in western New York in the 1920s and is about, in part, taxidermy.

"I'm not sure how many taxidermy experts there are left in the world," Scott responds to my question. "Probably not too many."

Besides writing *The Manikin*, Scott has broadened the focus of her work over the past few years. She wrote a two-act play titled *Speakeasy* that was produced and performed in 1995 by the Todd Theater Troupe at the University of Rochester and with a small cast at LaMama in New York City. "I took the central part of the story from an article written by Edmund Wilson titled 'The Dorothy Perkins Story' about a seventeen-year-old girl who shot and killed her fiancé at a Valentine's Day party. The trial became a sensation because she was young and beautiful and in danger of being sent to the electric chair."

Scott also interviewed South African novelist J. M. Coetzee for the *Paris Review*.[1] "He had been interviewed many times before, and the challenge for me was to try to explore something new with him. I discussed the action of his prose and the transformation of ideas into fiction. I also engaged him in conversation about the craft of writing."

In addition to these two projects, Scott has also published several book reviews and an essay.

Scott works in a converted, second-floor sun porch in the single-family home she shares with husband James Longenbach and daughter Kathryn in Rochester's Pinnacle Hill section. She writes her initial drafts in longhand, usually starting early in the morning and continuing until around one. She begins by revising for a few hours before moving on to new work. "Most of my first drafts are barely legible due to the constant revising I do," she says.

After completing a draft she types it into her computer which she uses for editing the final drafts.

But not all of Scott's writing finds a reading audience. She has set aside many pieces of fiction that did not develop as she had planned, some of which were several hundred pages long. One particularly difficult period for Scott came after she finished *Arrogance*. "I kept writing in the same fragmented structure and felt I'd be writing books like it for the rest of my life. I ended up throwing out all of the work I did during the following year or so. Then I began to concentrate on the shorter fiction that was included in *Various Antidotes*, and this, finally, helped me to move in a new direction."

Scott wants to continue to stretch the boundaries of her fictional forms. This does not come as a surprise considering that some of her literary influences include Samuel Beckett, William Gass, and Salman Rushdie. Reading the manuscript of Rushdie's *Shame* while working at the Elaine Markson Literary Agency, Scott was inspired by his bold mix of fable and history. She wants her work to respond to the problems and needs of the contemporary world even as she turns to the past and reimagines it. The plans that she has for her writing also seem to resemble her own experiences—how the responsibilities and concerns of her work and family affect her life. "I want to play with structure, the idea of interruption, telling different stories in the same piece, digressing," she says. "How's that for a wrap-up answer?"

Notes

1. The interview with J. M. Coetzee ended up being published in *Salmagundi*.

Voice and Trajectory: An Interview with J. M. Coetzee

Joanna Scott / 1997

From *Salmagundi*, no. 114/115 (Spring–Summer 1997): 82–102. Reprinted by permission.

Joanna Scott: Let's begin with your early impressions of South Africa. What significant things in your education shaped you as a writer of fiction?
J. M. Coetzee: If you mean my education, strictly speaking, if you mean what I learned in educational institutions, the answer must be, nothing. All that my schooling taught me was pity for children, or for some of them—for those who could not cope with—what shall we call it?—the educational experience.

JS: Why pity? What did those children lose because of their education?
JMC: It's not so much a question of what they lost as of the deformations they underwent. The system was authoritarian. It taught obedience. Obedience was, in a sense, its real subject-matter. Most it cowed; some it turned into bullies.

JS: What were your impressions of the country as a child?
JMC: I could have no idea of an alternative to the environment in which I lived, so what impressions I had can't, logically speaking, count as impressions of this country. They were just impressions of life. And by now they have been recalled, revisited, revised so often that I can hardly claim with any confidence that they belong to my childhood. They belong, by now, to the childhood I have constructed for myself in retrospect, that is, to autobiography.

JS: What are some important aspects of that constructed autobiography, then?

JMC: A huge question. My relation to my parents. My relation to wider kinfolk. My relation to South African society, in all its fragmentedness (linguistic, ethnic, racial). My relation to language, in particular to English, the language I write in, and to the history embedded in that language.

JS: Your first direction was toward science. Why?
JMC: No, not toward science, toward mathematics. I didn't have any aptitude for science—physics, chemistry, biology, that kind of thing. No, I liked mathematics. I studied mathematics at university and from there went into computers. But I was not a creative mathematician. As I discovered (rather too late), I had no real talent.

JS: Why did you choose mathematics?
JMC: For the fun of it. I was attracted by the pleasures it offered. As, if I had known about chess early enough, I might have chosen to devote myself to chess.

JS: Are there aspects of fiction that give similar pleasure?
JMC: Yes: play. Mathematics is a kind of play, intellectual play. I've never been much interested in its applications, in the ways in which mathematics can be set to work. Play is, to me, one of the defining characteristics of human beings. I look askance at the word "work." When people talk of work I ask myself: What is going to be betrayed, sacrificed, in the name of work?

JS: You're generally suspicious of language. Are you suspicious of the word "play," too?
JMC: I'm suspicious of formulas of language that have hardened and set, that people believe in without question. I'm not aware that this settling of opinion has happened to the concept of play. In fact, I'm not aware that anyone talks much about play nowadays. A pity.

JS: You've written an essay in which you compare children's play to textual play. One thing that struck me in that essay was your discussion of how play, even for children, becomes regulated, so they lose a sense of spontaneity or creativity.
JMC: Yes, that's so. There's a kind of creative play—inventing games rather than just playing games—that I find very precious, one of the most precious things about childhood. Too many people who write about childhood—Freud, for instance—try to turn play into work. To Freud, play is evidence of

the work that the unconscious is doing. Is there any theory of play in Freud? I suspect not. There's not much theory of play anywhere that I can think of.

JS: I guess the fort-da discussion is about control.
JMC: Yes, adaptive work.

JS: Since your years in the PhD program at Austin, you've remained distinctly interested in literary theory. Other critics have taken that interest and applied it to your fiction. Elsewhere you've spoken about how these are two different forms of intellectual activity for you and don't have much to do with each other. So what happens when they are connected by critics?
JMC: In this respect—with respect to what other people have to say about my fiction—my overriding criterion, I'm afraid, has to be: Is this good for me? Is this good for me to read, is this good for me to know, is this good for me to think about? My conclusion is usually that there is no advantage in thinking too much about what others write about me. So not only don't I know the answer to your question, but in a deeper, strategic sense I'm not interested in the answer.

JS: At Austin you wrote a thesis on Beckett. How has Beckett influenced your fiction?
JMC: I have great admiration for Beckett, particularly the Beckett of the middle period. Beckett criticism nowadays is more interested in the last phase of his career. The last phase—I'm not sure what to think about it. But I'm not fond of it. However, in my early twenties I read the books of the middle phase, which runs from *Watt*, composed during the war, through *The Unnameable*, but probably does not include *How It Is* (I see *How It Is* as a rerun of part of *The Unnameable*)—I read those books over and over again. That kind of close, repeated reading tends to influence the cadences of one's prose and perhaps even one's habits of thinking.

JS: When did you decide to start writing fiction? Can you describe the origins of *Dusklands*?
JMC: I had written a fair amount of poetry as an undergraduate in Cape Town, and later while I was living in London, but no fiction, though I had ambitions in that direction. I made my preparations by reading in the British Museum: accounts of early travel and exploration in South Africa. I was collecting material, as I thought novelists had to do. This reading continued in Texas, which had a very good library where I made all kinds of interesting discoveries. But the actual writing of *Dusklands* didn't begin until

January 1, 1970, when I was living in Buffalo. It was a New Year's resolution: to stop thinking and planning and actually start writing. *Dusklands* grew out of my interest in eighteenth-century South Africa, which has of late been the object of a lot of academic research, but in those days was a pretty much neglected historical period—out of my interest in the colonization of southern Africa and the role of my ancestors in that colonization. Out of that interest grew one half of the book, "The Narrative of Jacobus Coetzee." The other half, "The Vietnam Report," grew out of my feelings about what was going on in Vietnam. Because I lived in the United States while it was a country at war, those feelings could not be other than intense.

JS: You were arrested in an anti-war demonstration on the SUNY Buffalo Campus. What happened?

JMC: I was indeed arrested in Buffalo at the height of the anti-war demonstrations in 1970, but not in an anti-war demonstration as such. Along with some thirty colleagues from the faculty, I took part in a protest against the way in which our university—SUNY-Buffalo—was being led, that is to say, by a president who quartered hundreds of police officers on campus and retreated from his office to a secret bunker. This was not, in our view, a responsible way in which to run a university: it created a highly charged atmosphere in which teaching and learning were impossible. My colleagues and I went to the president's office one Sunday morning and refused to leave until he agreed to come and meet with us. He didn't come. Instead, he sent in the police. We were arrested, charged with trespassing, and convicted. A year later, on appeal, the conviction was overturned. That's the history.

JS: At some point you applied for your green card—was it because a teaching opportunity arose, or because you wanted to leave South Africa?

JMC: Because I wanted not to go back to South Africa.

JS: Why?

JMC: Because it was not an appealing place. Particularly then, in 1970. I had children too, and didn't want them educated in South Africa.

JS: But you did go back.

JMC: Yes. My application failed.

JS: How do you feel about that now?

JMC: What does one say? If I had stayed in the United States, I would by now have been a different person. I would have a different history. I wouldn't be here answering your questions.

JS: You use your surname in *Dusklands* and implicate yourself not just in the colonial history of South Africa but in the construction of the two fictions. Did you feel at all wary of, as your character Dawn says, "the persistent pressure of your imagination"?

JMC: The simple answer to your question is, no, I did not feel wary about what I was doing. But that is not to say I would do the same today. There are moments in both the novellas where I break with the conventions of verisimilitude in ways that are finally rather uninteresting. Or, to put it another way, there are "experiments" in *Dusklands* that are gestured at but not carried through productively. Among these half-baked experiments I would not, however, number making my remote ancestor Jacobus Coetzee a central figure, or indeed creating a fictional father to give his blessing to the project in a preface.

JS: Did you think of the two narratives as a novel?

JMC: The two narratives have a relation at the level of ideas, but otherwise the relation is loose. Is it so loose that the two parts might as well be separate publications? I don't know. I don't want to dodge your question, but a novel is ultimately nothing but a prose fiction of a certain length. It has no formal requirements to satisfy; to that extent, the question of whether X or Y is "really" a novel can't be very interesting. By itself, "The Narrative of Jacobus Coetzee" is no more and no less of a novel than, say, *A Journal of the Plague Year*, where Defoe also invested some energy in faking an authentic record.

JS: Like *Robinson Crusoe* or *Don Quixote*.

JMC: Yes. Considerable effort went into making the reader believe that the *Journal of the Plague Year* was written in the 1660s, and just as much energy went into faking *Robinson Crusoe*. As a result of which there are people all over the world who believe that *Robinson Crusoe* was written by Robinson Crusoe. Something like the same is true for *Dusklands*. There are people who believe not only that there was an explorer named Jacobus Coetzee, but that he wrote a narrative of his travels, which I translated.

JS: And you regret that pretense now?

JMC: No, I don't regret it, not at all. My reservations about the book are simply that there are a few things in the book that don't come off, little pieces of cleverness.

JS: The novel has been treated as an important response or reaction to certain conventions of realism. Is it a book that reacts to the inadequacies of realism?

JMC: Let's not talk about inadequacies, not even historically. Let's not say that realism was adequate to reality in the 1850s but is no longer adequate to reality in the 1970s—that's not the way it is. Let's just say that a certain renovation is necessary from generation to generation. By the 1960s the conventions of the kind of novel that was being written at the time—at least in South Africa—were very tired indeed. These were the conventions dominating British fiction as well. There was a general dissatisfaction and a search for new models. The new models looked at tended to be American. *Dusklands* was representative of that wave, rather than being particularly unique.

JS: It's both of those, isn't it?

JMC: Well, it's unique only in the sense that lots of other books being written around the same time were unique, or "unique." It was an inventive time.

JS: Your comment about cleverness—are you referring to self-reflexive tricks of narrative? Do you regret your participation in this experimental wave?

JMC: If I used the word regret, it's certainly not the best word. If I were doing the book over again (which is impossible, and why should I want to, anyway?), there would be pages I'd do differently. My doubts are not at the level of the word or phrase, not at the level of the overall conception, just at the level of the page.

JS: Could you comment on your manipulation of single voices, and your interest in Bakhtin's concept of "dialogism"?

JMC: Dialogism? More and more I suspect I don't understand the concept. The more I reread Bakhtin, the less I'm sure what dialogism is. Not, I think, because Bakhtin doesn't know what he means, but because there's something he's assuming in the way of shared cultural knowledge, specifically of Russian literature and maybe of Russian philosophy, that I don't have and very likely most of the people who take over the term dialogism from him don't have either. That's why I hesitate to answer your question.

JS: Why are you drawn to the monologue form?

JMC: Again, bear in mind that monologue is not necessarily monological, if I understand Bakhtin. Nor is dialogue dialogical. There's a certain kind of monologue in which voices are evoked and contested and played with that is part of the dialogical. So if I'm interested in monologue, it's not just at a formal level. On the other hand, it's not at the level of whatever it is Bakhtin is talking about, which, I suspect, is finally a religious level.

JS: There's a change from *Dusklands* to *In the Heart of the Country.* The instability of Magda's voice is such a contrast to the assertiveness—especially of Jacobus. There's a broken quality to the voice. The voice starts to create its own pace. I'm interested in how you made that step, from the more assertive voices of *Dusklands* to the more self-reflective voice of Magda.

JMC: Do we ever know how we manage things? As you must have experienced yourself, such elements as tempo, voice, character don't come one by one, in sequence, they come all together. Character is voice, and voice is scene construction. I think at the formal level, the enabling device in *In the Heart of the Country* turned out to be the numbering of the sections, because that enabled me to drop all pretense of continuity. After a few hundred words of prose, there comes a break—a three-digit number. As a reader you can't lose yourself in the represented. But once, as a writer, you have given up on the possibility of continuity, of the reader's absorption, then all kinds of benefits flow. Like radical juxtapositions. Like going over the same story twice, but in different forms. So, yes, several things came together: a certain scene construction, a certain persona, a certain voice.

JS: I'm reminded of a comment that your fictional Foe makes about himself as a writer needing to post signs, or flags, in order not to be lost in the maze of doubt. So in a sense, the numbers did that for you? Grounded you in some way?

JMC: No. The numbers don't point anywhere.

JS: How did the numbers serve as an enabling device?

JMC: They enable a certain sharpness of transition, or lack of smooth transition. So much of one's time in continuous writing is spent on smoothing transitions from paragraph to paragraph. That smoothing-out process in prose is much like rhyming in verse: despite whatever new may be occurring in the line, it rhymes with the previous line or the line before that. Rhyme fosters continuity—as, I suppose, does meter. When you break up the surface of the prose, that soothing continuity can be forgotten.

JS: How did you invent the character of Magda (or perhaps we should call her a voice)? What did you start with? How extensive were the notes you took? What did you know about this character? What did you plan for her?

JMC: You're right to talk about her as a voice. Magda is coextensive with her voice—there's nothing "in" her that isn't in the voice, in the words. As for what I knew about her, I have no idea. I certainly didn't know who she was before she started talking, nor do I know what happened to her after she stopped talking. I don't take notes from real life in the manner of, say, Zola.

JS: There are no notes? But you've spoken of notes you've made for your novels.

JMC: Yes, notes about historical events, topography, rainfall figures—that kind of thing. And I make notes about work in progress or work in prospect. But I don't make notes on people I've met or listened to and feel I must incorporate into books.

JS: Magda tells us that she's stuck inside the maze of her monologue. She doesn't learn to control her situation or to communicate. She achieves no intimacy through language. So do we consider her stuck in language?

JMC: That may be the way she sees it. But the fact is, she's a considerable verbal artist, whatever we mean by "she." It may be a maze she's stuck in, but she herself built it.

JS: You did make her a "she." What does it mean for you to take on a female voice?

JMC: A complicated question. One way of responding is to ask, is one, as a writer, at every level, sexed? Is there not a level where one is, if not pre-sexual, then anterior to sex? First anterior to sex, then becoming sexed? At that level, or in that transition between levels, does one actually "take on" the voice of another sex? Doesn't one "become" another sex? On the other hand, I must ask myself, who is this "one" who is anterior to Magda?

JS: What are the repercussions of gender? What effect does it have on the narrative, or on the style?

JMC: An interesting question, because the language of *In the Heart* . . . is not soft, not rounded. So some of the more obvious marks of the feminine that might have been worked into it just aren't there. When the book came out, I was prepared for comments of the kind, "She doesn't sound like a woman"—like a "real" woman. But those comments didn't come; I don't know why.

JS: Did the opposite comments come? Were you praised for the authenticity of your female voice?

JMC: Not in so many words, but I know of at least one woman who took the story to heart to the extent of reading it as a retelling, in other terms, of her own life story. And took it to heart to the extent of wanting to make it her own by doing a film of the book, which she eventually brought off. Not, incidentally, a South African but a Belgian. It wasn't as though the events of Magda's life recalled the events of her life. It is rather that there was something in the voice that she took as her own.

JS: Can you describe how you write and revise? How does the process of revision open to the process of writing and invention?

JMC: Obviously, no one begins by saying, A) I'm going to write a novel on the following subject, and B) I'm going to write it the following way. Method is not distinct from subject. What the novelist does in each case is his or her method.

JS: Or what we've done.

JMC: Or what we've done, what we did the last time—exactly. One of the things to be thankful for, although maybe one needs to be suspicious of it too, is that writing gets easier—becomes almost a way of life. Blessedly, you don't have to invent everything from scratch all over again. But to answer your question: I write in longhand, until I don't know what to write next. And then I go back over it and maybe type it out. And hope that in the process I will find out what it is I need to do next.

JS: How much will you write out in longhand before you start to type it out?

JMC: Oh, I don't know, maybe two hundred pages.

JS: So you write straight through for two hundred pages?

JMC: We're talking in generalities. And we're not counting false starts.

JS: Do you have finished narratives that you've thrown out or put in a drawer?

JMC: No, I don't. Not yet.

JS: I know your books were never banned, but I'm struck by the representation of violence in your novels, which seems to me politically charged, given the situation in South Africa. It surprises me that your books slipped in through the censorship laws of the seventies. Maybe by *Waiting for the Barbarians* the laws had relaxed a bit.

JMC: No, they hadn't. When *Waiting for the Barbarians* came out, the thaw was just about to set in. It's not as though my books slipped through the net without being read by the censors. In at least one case there was an order to the Customs to detain the book. So my inference is that they were read and passed.

One has to remember the way in which the system operated. There were so-called reading committees, on which there would typically be clergymen, retired teachers, custodians of culture—that kind of sector of Afrikaans society. These reading committees were set up more or less according to the convenience of the members of the committee, and were assigned books—at least novels—more or less at random to read. So there was always something a little hit-or-miss about the system. To put it another way, it was not a system of censorship such as you would set up in an ideal dystopia. Some books got bad committees, some books got good committees. Some books that were by any reckoning innocuous got banned. Probably I was the other side of the coin.

JS: Were you consciously writing around the censorship laws?
JMC: If you really mean consciously, then the question you have posed is a moral one. Was I playing along with the censorship laws? How can you expect me to say, Yes, I was?

JS: I don't see it as playing along at all. I see it as subversive.
JMC: Well, I know about the tricks that were used in places like Russia and Poland to get around the censors. You'd use aesopian references, code words that your select readership would pick up but that the censors would be blind to. But in my view that too constitutes playing the game, even if it means playing against rather than playing with. Anyway, the aesopian method assumes an extraordinary community of interest between readers and writers of the kind that you might get among an embattled intelligentsia in Russia or Poland, but that you absolutely would not get in South Africa. The readership there is not sophisticated enough.

JS: Because of poor literacy? What do you mean by "sophisticated"?
JMC: No, I'm not referring to literacy, not in the usual sense. Russian readers, from early in the nineteenth century, learned to pick up hints and allusions and nuances. It was this competency in following a subtext that did much to define them as a reading community. A community of readers in that sense has never yet come into being in South Africa.

JS: And yet your books, with their structural play and complicated language, seem written for readers experienced in strategies of ambiguity.
JMC: That may or may not be so. But readers, even a number of readers, do not themselves constitute a reading community.

JS: You've been working in a different genre lately—you're talking with a film company here about a project?
JMC: There's an independent production company interested in filming *Waiting for the Barbarians.* It is necessarily a larger production than *In the Heart of the Country,* simply because of the scale on which the action takes place. A larger production, a more expensive production, more money has to be raised, raising the money is more of an effort. The film *In the Heart of the Country* was done on a medium-sized Belgian government grant, with very respectable actors. I saw the film by chance on Swiss television recently, so it's still doing the rounds.

JS: Your interest in montage as a narrative technique in *In the Heart of the Country*—were you looking to cinema for variations?
JMC: This is something I talk about at length in *Doubling the Point,* where I probably express myself better than I can now. There are specific films, films of a particular kind, that I was using as a model. I mean films in which there's a certain combination of stills, voice-over, and moving picture, used in combination.

JS: Another narrative challenge you've mentioned elsewhere is the challenge of describing an unfamiliar landscape in *Waiting for the Barbarians.* What kinds of challenges did you face?
JMC: Let me be clearer. In *Waiting for the Barbarians* the challenge was not to describe or represent an unfamiliar landscape. It was to construct a landscape, a landscape that I've never seen and that probably doesn't exist. Construct or perhaps even fake it. It was necessary because, inter alia, *Barbarians* is a book that uses the seasons to set moods in quite a traditional way.

JS: Could you talk about the genesis of the book more generally?
JMC: I tend to go blank on geneses. I simply don't remember how books I have written started off. Part of the reason is that the beginnings generally get abandoned during the course of revision. If there's an archeology of the book, then the beginnings are deep under the surface, under the soil.

JS: Is there a point when you know something is a viable project?

JMC: Yes, there is: when I've invested so much time in it that I can't afford to stop, can't afford to face the fact that I've wasted six months of my life, or whatever. So I soldier on, and the book gets written.

JS: In *White Writing*, you've written about the failure of the pastoral tradition. Where does *Waiting for the Barbarians* fit in to, or outside of, the tradition?

JMC: I've never thought of those two books in conjunction. But I don't think it's a useful lead. By about page five of the novel it's evident that the pastoral dream is no longer viable. There may have been a pastoral age, but it ended long before the book begins.

JS: But doesn't the Magistrate continue to yearn for an Edenesque past?

JMC: Well, so what?

JS: In that sense, it continues through the book. The past remains an object of desire.

JMC: We're saying slightly different things. The books I was writing about in *White Writing*—books by other South African novelists—are efforts to construct imaginary pastoral worlds, imaginary worlds that don't happen to work as blueprints for the real world. That's what I understand the failure of the pastoral generally to be: a failure to be realizable. *Barbarians* is a novel about a man who, in bad times, keeps harking back to a pastoral past. That isn't the same thing as trying to erect a pastoral model.

JS: Is there something dangerous or deceptive about the desire to look back to a purer time?

JMC: Dangerous? I don't think so, no. It's built into the Christian worldview, and into Christian mythology, that there was a good time before everything got so bad. It's a feature of other religions too, maybe of religious thinking in general: things used to be better once upon a time.

JS: Then it's comforting nostalgia.

JMC: Is it? Nostalgia isn't just comforting. Nostalgia is a very complex emotion. In a sense, it provides a sort of pillow to rest your head on. But at the same it reminds you of something lost, something you don't have.

JS: Returning to the idea of the pastoral in *White Writing*, you discuss the failure of the landscape literature to find a language that is authentically African. Could you say more about that?

JMC: That comment is less interesting than it may seem at first glance, because the irony is of course that there are plenty of authentically African languages in which to talk about the African landscape, namely, African languages. These are not only languages without a European past but languages of cultures that don't have a scenic tradition. So the uninteresting irony is that there were languages available, but if the writers in question had been able to move into these languages and make use of them, they would probably have lost their scenic ambitions as well.

JS: I wonder what sort of reaction you've had to the review by Anthony Burgess that described *Waiting for the Barbarians* as a book that "is not about anywhere and hence it is about everywhere." Such a comment calls to mind the sticky issue of allegory.

JMC: I didn't see the review but I certainly read the quote when someone at Viking Penguin stuck it on the back of the book. Allegory is not, of course, about everywhere: it's just about somewhere else. I've always been slightly bemused by the description of me as an allegorist, but maybe I know less than other people do.

JS: In your own review of Mahfouz's *The Harafish*, you describe the realist novel as a "vehicle of Europe's bourgeoisie." Much has been done with this idea of the novel as a middle-class form, but your comment sounds very bitter. Do you see yourself as subverting or countering that tradition?

JMC: It seems to me very late to be coming on the scene today as a subverter of the realist novel. No, I think if there's any subversion of the realist novel it was done in *Ulysses*, which is now seventy-odd years old. There's a good deal of truth in the account of realism—in England, at any rate—that situates it within the rise of the middle class. As you know, the famous book is the one by Ian Watt, *The Rise of the Novel*. It dates from the 1950s, and has been queried on details, sometimes large details, but as long as one doesn't generalize too far from the group of novelists Watt was writing about, I think its outlines remain very firm. But the history of realism isn't continuous. The realist novel gets invented and reinvented. There's no clear line leading from England in the eighteenth century to France in the mid-nineteenth century. The French reinvent realism in a different form.

But it's still very much tied up with the middle class, though now in an embroiled, antagonistic way.

JS: I don't want to continue this if this isn't a direction you want to go in, but the kinds of divisions made in South Africa between social realism and modernist or experimental fiction are angry divisions. How do you negotiate that as a writer?
JMC: Three comments. One: it isn't in my interest, as I understand my interest, to get involved in polemics. Two: pronouncements about how the novel should be written strike me as more typical of the cultural—how shall I say, I want to avoid the phrase cultural commissar—the cultural spokesperson than of the writer. Three, and perhaps more interestingly: the particularly strident polemic you mention between social realism and so-called experimental or modernist or even postmodernist fiction is largely obsolete now—obsolete largely because no one ever produced a social realist South African novel, just as in the Soviet Union no one ever produced a social realist novel that anyone was prepared to read. Thankfully, the debate has shifted into a more nuanced and complex mode.

JS: Can we talk about *Foe*? What brought you to Defoe in such an encompassing way? You didn't just write about him, you wrote out of him, out of his novel.
JMC: I hope I'm a serious reader, and being a serious reader may mean that you get absorbed into the writing project of someone who is larger than yourself. It happened to me with Defoe, it happened with Dostoevsky, and—who knows?—it may happen again.

JS: But why Defoe? Why that writer?
JMC: Because Defoe is a fascinating and absorbing writer. Part of his fascination is that he is so uninterested in standing back and reflecting upon and judging what he's doing. He's just a writer. He writes.

JS: You construct an intricate frame around Susan's voice in the novel. Most of the time she doesn't speak directly. She is quoted by Foe. I wonder what thoughts you have in retrospect about the various shapes of her voice?
JMC: *Foe* is a novel I haven't looked at since I wrote it ten years ago, so my memory may have to be jogged. I suppose you are right—I remember lots of nesting quote marks, voices within voices. I remember feeling a lot of affec-

tion for Susan Barton, by the end, and wondering why I never got to meet her. What people call confusing the real and the imaginary.

JS: Who is speaking at the end of the novel? I'm not sure I know. Is it the author? A narrator?
JMC: Goodness knows. I don't know.

JS: *The Master of Petersburg* puts Dostoevsky at the center. Why did you choose that historical time?
JMC: It was a time—we're talking about the late 1860s—when he was struggling with the composition of a book, not knowing what it was going to be about, just knowing it had to be a big book. In fact he tried to write at least three different books using the same material—material in an abstract rather than concrete sense. The book that eventually emerged was *The Possessed.* The record of that period is absorbing and very humbling to follow. My novel takes up that period and reimagines it, so to speak.

JS: Was part of the attraction an identification you felt with Dostoevsky?
JMC: With Dostoevsky? Who's to know? But it doesn't look that way to me. There's a great deal about Dostoevsky, starting with the fact that he's Russian, that is absolutely foreign to me.

JS: It sounds like that difference might have made the fictional leap easier.
JMC: That's possible. The difference may indeed make the leap easier to take. Of course it doesn't guarantee that you won't fall on your face, trying to write out of a world that is so unfamiliar.

JS: Did you go to Russia to do research for the novel?
JMC: I've never been to Russia.

JS: You change historical facts and shift dates in the novel. It's odd that this should be a concern at this point in time, given the general irreverence of novelists. But responses to *The Master of Petersburg* suggest that it is a concern.
JMC: Not my concern. In *The Possessed* the names of personages are not historical names and the identities are not historical identities. Yet no one is going to say that *The Possessed* is not about the Russia of 1870. It's not as though Dostoevsky himself does not imagine or reimagine history, imagine or reimagine the scene around him.

JS: You place Pavel's death at an earlier date. Was this a necessary reinvention, an essential element of your fiction? Or did you do it because you wanted to say something about history and the dominance of fiction over history?

JMC: The death of Pavel brings Dostoevsky face to face with Nechaev, which is something that didn't happen in real life, so to that extent it allows me to engineer a meeting between two very important historical figures.

JS: Could you talk about your use of history in general? You've made some comments about the novel as a rival to history. Is it an antagonistic relationship? David Attwell redefines it as complementary.

JMC: David Attwell is of course operating with concerns of his own. I would prefer to retain the word rivalry. There can be rivalries of various kinds, but when the crunch comes, the relation between history and fiction is still a rivalrous one. People say that discursive models in the human sciences are giving way to narrative models. I know of a few instances, principally from anthropology and archeology. But these instances don't persuade me that the grand discourses have yet been abandoned in favor of narrative—narrative with all its implications understood and embraced and appreciated (that's worth underlining).

JS: What are the implications of fictional narrative?

JMC: I can't make an exhaustive list, but they do include abandoning the support that comes with a certain institutional voice, the voice of the historian or sociologist or whatever. It entails no longer being an expert, no longer being master of your discourse.

JS: There seem to be intense rivalries within the discipline of history in South Africa. Historians are debating not only what should be an appropriate subject for history, but how to represent the past as well.

JMC: It's a huge question not only within South Africa but at a theoretical level as well. It is usually presented in terms of decentering the narrative of history. But decentering strikes me as a rather negative move. There ought to be other ways of thinking about it.

JS: In *The Life and Times of Michael K*, Michael tries to find refuge from the war in his solitude. Yet in *Age of Iron*, Mrs. Curren blames herself for only "half-attending" to the violence in South Africa; eventually, she is compelled to participate. Could you comment on these different responses to violence?

JMC: Novels engage with particularities. From a certain distance Michael K and Elizabeth Curren may both be seen as responding to what you call violence. But in fact they are two people at different moments in history acting out of complexes of pressures and desires that are quite individual and which set them far apart. My fidelity is ultimately to them and for their unique plights, not to any grand historical trajectory they may be seen as belonging to.

JS: Do you see these two novels as visionary fictions? Are they, in some sense, warnings?

JMC: Once again, it's not my task, not the onus laid upon me, to slot my novels into compartments. From one angle, they may look like one thing—warnings, for instance; from another angle, at another time, they may look quite different.

JS: In your recent collection of essays, *Giving Offense*, you comment on "the decline of the book" and the dominance of electronic media. What are the foreseeable consequences of this decline for you, as a novelist?

JMC: *Giving Offense* is about censorship. Therefore, much of the time, it looks at books from the perspective of the censoring authority, of the state. What I point out is fairly obvious: that in an age in which electronic forms of communication have become dominant, print, and particularly print in book form, is read by too few people to create much anxiety in the state. (It was a measure of the technological backwardness of the old Soviet Union that, well into the 1980s, it continued to take writers seriously enough to persecute them.) Until recently South Africa too was backward enough, or deliberately made itself backward enough, to take books seriously and, on occasion, ban them. Now all that has changed. South Africa has joined the world, books are no longer banned. They are also no longer taken seriously. Am I disappointed? To a degree. On the other hand, I have never been entirely persuaded that writers are the unacknowledged legislators of mankind.

Joanna Scott Interviews Maureen Howard

Joanna Scott / 1998

This interview, Maureen Howard by Joanna Scott, was commissioned by and first published in *Bomb*, no. 63, Spring 1998. © Bomb Magazine, New Art Publications, and its Contributors. Allrights reserved. The BOMB Digital Archive can be viewed at www.bombmagazine.org.

Enter the living room of Maureen Howard's Upper West Side apartment, and you will find yourself surrounded by pieces of the world. Huge pine cones decorate the mantel. Woven paisley shawls have been tucked with subtle care over the arms of the chaise and the sofa. In the dining room, the walls are covered with prints of jesters, clowns, acrobats. Half a dozen individual brass candlesticks stand in an uneven circle in the center of the long table, looking like a group of guests who have just stopped dancing and are waiting for the music to begin again. Enter the fiction of Maureen Howard, and you find yourself surrounded by pieces of the world. She is an inventor who shapes her creations from found things, from the bric-à-brac of history—orange pencils (number two), gin and bitters, Georgian silver, rubber flip flops, angel food cake decorated with miniature American flags.

In her new novel, *A Lover's Almanac* (Viking), she invents a fictional winter in the year 2000, and follows two sets of lovers, young and old, as they stagger away from the twentieth century. Using the embracing form of the almanac to shape her novel, Maureen draws anecdotes and paradoxes from such historical figures as Benjamin Franklin, William James, and Gertrude Stein, mixing the diverse voices to explore the effects of hindsight and the illusions of prophecy. Her characters must look backward in order to go forward into the next millennium. Memory, Maureen suggests, gives shape to the mysterious future. On the morning of the last day of 1997, I sat with Maureen in her dining room and talked with her about the past, the future, and her fiction. I've known Maureen for five years—she's gracious and witty and can set anyone at ease. But to tell the truth, I felt myself growing tense as we prepared to begin this conversation. At first I thought the tape recorder was making me nervous, giving me the sensation that we were being watched. But then I realized that we *were* being watched by one of Maureen's own things—a contortionist in a print on the wall, the figure bending in and out and around in order to look back at us from between his legs and dare, *Now you try!* And so we began—

Joanna Scott: In *A Lover's Almanac* you quote William James: "In point of fact all stories end." So, let's go back to the beginning of this novel. What prompted you, what sent you into the fiction?

Maureen Howard: I began with the idea of an almanac. I suppose that idea grew out of a section of my earlier book, *Natural History*, which has about it a notebook quality, a way of collecting history that was at once related to and separate from the narrative. My draw to the almanac began with the *Old Farmer's Almanac*, the little yellow book that you can buy in the supermarket, with a section that says how to predict the future accurately every time.

JS: Every time?

MH: Every time. It has about it a most wonderful sense of fact. The tides, the heavens. Walt Whitman made fun of the "learned astronomer," but this learned astronomer makes sure that his facts are accurate. The almanac is very much a modern popular form, yet it's been around for a long time. The Egyptians, the Incas, carefully calculated their almanacs, which were also religious texts. When the almanac got into the hands of Benjamin Franklin, it became wildly popular, a great best-seller. Of course, Franklin intruded his own story, his aphorisms: puzzles, entertainments, how to live, what to cook in season. He expanded the almanac into the fictional as well as the factual. I was very taken with the form. I believe it works for the problems that we face having to do with belief, disbelief, with indeterminacy and determinacy. See what I mean?

JS: You've found the perfect form for blending fact and fiction. It gives you the freedom to move so liberally through the narrative, in and out of the characters' stories, into the past, into the future. The form suits the genre so well, since the novel loves to incorporate so many different types of discourse.

MH: When you think back, let's say to George Eliot, or Dickens, the nineteenth-century novel, surely these were writers who had confidence to stop and tell us what they were about. About prisons, about matters of whaling and rigging and politics.

JS: I noticed you begin the book with a quote from *Moby Dick*. I think you share with Melville the love of another compendium, the encyclopedia. Yet novelists have always been ambivalent about facts. Certainly facts that present themselves as true are important to your work, but you're making the story, you're changing facts, playing with them.

MH: Yes, to question, to doubt the standard version, so there is a semblance of being able to control the whole spill of history. And what can you do with that semblance? You gather the facts, you say: Here is history. But how can we make it something less cool, less distant? How can we take it into ourselves? We can in the novel. Just as the almanac accommodates to fancy and information, to astrology and astronomy, the novel enlarges the field of play to use facts, and to confront them.

JS: The novel has often positioned itself as a true document. Think back to the way Defoe offers his *Robinson Crusoe* as a found text. The need to claim that fiction is true, seems to me, to have both invigorated and haunted the novel.

MH: There is that statement in Cervantes, in which Sancho says to Don Quixote that he does not believe everything the master says. And that recurs in Calvino in *Invisible Cities*. The emperor does not always believe the Marco Polo story.

JS: *A Lover's Almanac* is very much a book about how to tell stories, how the rough stuff of life is made into a shapely story. It seems true of your work from the start, that you've always been interested in blending forms, different kinds of narratives. But suddenly, in *Natural History*, we get major interruption: narratives drawn from other texts, histories that are more tangentially related and fascinating in themselves.

MH: Sometimes I think I wrote *Natural History* because I live down the street from the natural history museum. (*laughter*) The Museum of Natural History has dioramas which are both wonderful and spooky, those re-created scenes of native life in Africa and Asia. They are highly theatrical with beautiful, very real details of other worlds. I'm very interested in worlds other than our own. *Natural History* is my own dark diorama of the town I grew up in—Bridgeport, Connecticut. I tend to use different forms at once in a work, and I wanted that book to be layered. A fiction writer is an amateur archaeologist, who dusts away the layers to see what can be discovered. Dust would be the narrative interruptions, the shards you suddenly come across. And there are many layers to a name, to a place, which in my mind all connect finally to the story.

JS: When I was a child, I used to go to the Museum of Natural History, and as I looked at the wild animals, poised in attack or running through a field, lounging or leaping, whatever they were doing, I thought they had been killed and frozen in that position. I thought I was seeing the moment when the animal confronts the hunter. The action of the dioramas—for years I thought this was the action of dying.

MH: That's because you are blessed with never having disassociated completely from a child's imagination in your fiction.

JS: At one point in *A Lover's Almanac* you say, "Tolerant reader, I take the liberty of defending these aging children . . . they have not lived through wars." What does that mean to come from this postwar generation? Does history really shape a generation?

MH: Well, I think that not having lived through a war does shape a segment of the population. It has been brought up to me by my students when I'm talking about, let's say Virginia Woolf's *Between the Acts*, which is a war novel. Students say, "We don't understand that," and I think that's true. I hope they will tolerate my prim, frumpy, patronizing narrative voice saying, "Tolerant reader."

JS: It's obviously satirical.

MH: Yes, but it's just as true that my generation did not experience the heroics of the Second World War on home ground. The Civil War was the last military action of great consequence within this country, and it shaped us, as a nation politically for many years.

JS: You seem to resist what in another book you call the packaging of history: the "gay nineties," the "roaring twenties," the "sixties." No, you say, it's dangerous to speak of decades as though they were cereal boxes.

MH: It's parochial to speak of decades that way, as a foolish kind of packaging that disregards both the larger and the marginalized culture. When I ragged on decades in the novel *Expensive Habits*, the woman was trying to explain to her son what she had actually lived through; that is, what storytelling is about, telling where you've been to those who will come after. It's the mother writing her legacy for the son; that's also true in another book, *Before My Time*, in which an older woman hands the past to a miscreant boy caught in the sixties. The sixties come up again in *A Lover's Almanac*—the great failed romance. The yield was a lot less than any of us wanted it to be. Which, I suppose, is what this book is about. How we move on, track where we are.

JS: But here you've gone beyond where we are and set the story a few years ahead, significantly, at the turn of the millennium. I was curious about that. What new requirements did you suddenly have when you moved the fiction forward?

MH: One of the reasons why I wanted it to be millennial was because it's not quite true. There is all that much-debated business about the stars, and how the astronomers can fix the birth of Christ four years off from the calendar that we follow. And yet we believe the calendar to be absolutely accurate. Moving time ahead also released me into playing with stories within stories, what's currently going on in America and what might come about.

JS: There's a wonderful passage in your novel *Bridgeport Bus* in which you compare a story to a German Easter egg. We hold the egg, which contains these delicate scenes, we look at it, but while we're holding it, we also look at our hands, that's how you put it, the fleshiness of our fingers, the torn cuticles. So we're seeing our fingers, we're seeing the egg, we're seeing the fiction, and we're seeing ourselves as we read it. I feel in your work and especially in this new novel that I am very much seeing myself holding the book. There's an intense self-consciousness that makes me think about where I am in my life, where I am in history. Was that part of your intention?

MH: Yes, I was conscious of that double effect of story time and reading time in *Natural History* and more so in this book, and of making a book, its physical presence. Books will be with us for a long time. I'm perfectly happy with the fact that we are moving ahead. The computer screen is in its infancy in terms of what it will hold for writers and readers. I'm delighted with that. But—we still have the book. This almanac is my book made to give to readers, whoever they may be. There's that quote in *The Lover's Almanac*, that lovely thing from Walt Whitman, in the printing it yourself, binding it yourself, selling it on the street yourself. We don't do that ourselves these days. Unfortunately there's the corporate apparatus—though the folks at Viking are very down home. In the high-sixties we had something called penny poems, which people wrote and sold on the street eliminating the dealer, in order to connect one-on-one for a penny—I like that.

JS: It's a romantic idea. And maybe that's what the internet will give us too—we'll eliminate the dealer and pass our narratives around for a penny. You do talk in *A Lover's Almanac* about the novel as a bourgeois form: "that blowsy bourgeois form in which money is ever present."

MH: The novel evolved as a form in the eighteenth century because suddenly there was an audience and means of commercial distribution. Yes, it's so often noted the rise of the novel was connected to the rise of the middle class. Yeah, the blowsy form, a sense, even on the part of the writer that I'm co-opted into the system. Look what I'm doing, this performance, big production.

JS: But it's not. A few months ago you lent me the galleys of Hermione Lee's biography of Virginia Woolf. Not only did I read this wonderful biography, but I got to see the passages you marked and starred. One passage was about Virginia Woolf's love of reading, and how reading for her was like an intimate conversation, or an act of love. You marked that passage. I think there is very much an intimacy to your book. It's as if you reach your hand out of the book and say, "Reader, talk back to me. I want to have a conversation with you." So you ask us questions, you encourage us to dive in and interpret, and all the while to think about our place in this and compare the hand to the wonderfully intricate design in the egg.

MH: Yes, I want to connect. I would feel bereft finishing a book in which I hadn't strived for connection. And yet, reading—as in reading out loud to others, reading in what must have been a lovely way, when the serial of the next installment of Dickens or James came through—that is lost to us now. Reading is connection, and writing is connection, both intimate acts yet acts that are done alone though not lonely. Do you see what I mean?

JS: I do. You say you want to "connect." Now, every art form creates a different connection between audience and object, so can you describe the connection you feel both as a writer and as a reader too?

MH: I'm interested in voices. I like variation in voice, in tone. Sometimes, certainly in reading Virginia Woolf, the printed page has about it a tremendous musical effect, a composition in terms of the tone of the sentence, the crescendo of a paragraph. I love to hear that music and want very much to be able to incorporate, to tell stories like a minstrel. That great Dickens line—he does the police in different voices, it's enormously important to me as a writer to do the voices, and hope they will be heard.

JS: *Bridgeport Bus* ends with a single voice saying, "It is no great sin to be at last alone." Often you leave us with solitary voices. And yet I feel comforted by your fiction of solitude. It's not necessarily a despairing solitude as much as an acceptance of solitude.

MH: At the end of *Lover's Almanac*, both of the lovers who have finally found each other, settled into life, are still alone in their pursuit of what will come next.

JS: They go their separate ways for the day.

MH: They do. In that moment Lou feels she will paint again, though she may never do the big thing, but she gets back to work. And Artie goes back to his math and his science. It might be too late; like the pursuit of history was for his grandfather. They go back to that part of themselves, to their work, which can only be pursued alone. I just read, this very morning, a wonderful line that was quoted from Conrad, from *Heart of Darkness*, "We live as we dream, alone."

JS: Yeah, as we dream and as we write and as we read.

MH: True, but that doesn't necessarily mean that we have to step outside of the world of human connection.

JS: You're very much an urban writer, you write about the city, you write from the city. Your fiction is full of people wandering through Bridgeport, Connecticut, or New York City, looking for connections and accepting their place in the city. I wondered how much you need the city to write. Do you need it as other writers need to look at a certain image or listen to music in order to write?

MH: I want the city streets, I love the streets, I love the faces, the people, the hardness of the city, and then the miraculous moments of grace in that hardness. I grew up in a real city, which was a wonderful city at that time, and I think New York is wonderful and exhausting, exhausting in terms of the events that can be observed.

JS: How do you go about collecting those observances? How do you pick and choose?

MH: Perhaps as the result of having too many things around me, which I have in my life, what I have to do is orchestrate. I have to see how much I can thematically tie together, which is itself a fiction. One of the things about the city that interests me in this book is that there is so much we don't know. Sissy, that runaway child, we don't know her, unless we are her social worker. One of the tragedies of living in the cities in America is that we are isolated. It's wrong to say that we are savvy New Yorkers. I wish it were so, that we really knew those who we live amongst and that they knew us, but we don't. It's all too easy to let Sissy and Little Man become stereotypical runaways or druggie kids. Without even thinking, we make them background figures, and this is terribly unfair.

JS: Sissy does have one beautiful moment to savor, doesn't she? A moment that resonates.

MH: Yes, she kisses Artie, and the kiss means something to her but nothing to him.

JS: When I emerge from this book, I can't let go of any of these characters, and she's one of them. Yet we have to think about what we call these "peripheral lives." Why are they peripheral? Why can we so easily turn from those lives in order to maintain our own peaceful days?

MH: Despite all the good people working at soup kitchens or helping with literacy programs, there is still a tremendous distance, certainly for my characters. The characters themselves cannot make these connections, though they do sometimes in random intersections of life. But then there are some intersections that have consequences; stories are told, two lives meet. The old woman, Sylvie, finally tells the story she has withheld even from herself, of why she and her mother so abruptly left Austria, at the time of the Anschluss. She tells it to the young woman who has become family. There's a good deal in the book about false parents and parents that do not function as parents. Sylvie becomes a perfectly fine substitute mother.

JS: We are looking into the future at the end of the novel, but it's a celebration. To borrow your phrase, you give the blowsy bourgeois form a happy ending.

MH: Yes, I think it's a bit of a risk, but so what?

JS: How so?

MH: Come, come. One of the great received truths of the present is that of our disaffection, isn't it?

JS: Especially when we're talking about the millennia! (*laughter*)

MH: But if you think of Shakespeare's *Winter's Tale*, there is a bittersweet ending for young lovers and old. The reunions at the end are undercut by haunting problems of the past and doubts of the future. A romantic comedy—there is a marriage.

JS: Well, Artie and Lou actually don't get married, do they?

MH: No, they don't get married! (*laughter*) But it's a love story.

JS: Fiction comes out of the tradition of the romance, though now we use that word in a different way, in a way that's less interesting. You mean it as adventure.

MH: Yes, their romantic adventure is a quest of self-discovery for both the old and young lovers.

JS: *A Lover's Almanac* takes place during one season?

MH: Just one season.

JS: And the almanac is four seasons.

MH: If I'm granted the time, I'm going to write the four seasons. But not in almanac form; I do not think the form of this book, which I appropriated for winter, could possibly be sustained for four seasons, so I have quite other forms in mind for the other seasons. Spring will be three tales. I'm interested in the tale; I think the difference between story and tale is less familiar to us now than it was for Hawthorne and Poe.

JS: What is the difference?

MH: Tales can be much more magical. More mythic, yet strictly objective—told with their moral, their enchantment. I think that many of Angela Carter's stories are tales. I think that many of Joanna Scott's stories are tales.

JS: Does it mean to be more magical, to have more license to invent?

MH: Yes, and to tell a kind of romance which is very inventive, less bound to verisimilitude—summer is a pastoral. Then I thought it would be fun to do the last season as an Advent card.

JS: Oh, wonderful! With the chocolate inside. (*laughter*)

MH: With the chocolate inside and the little toys. They used to only advertise the religious; open the little flap and there's another angel or another bit of blessed information. Now you have to eat the chocolate to get to the religion. (*laughter*) We're very silly wanting constantly to be entertained. I'm distraught by how much we need to be entertained.

JS: But then you are working in an art form in which you are entertaining.
MH: I know, it's a bind.

JS: Do you want to change people?
MH: You mean change readers?

JS: Yes.
MH: The work may move people, but the idea is not to ask art to deliver a therapeutic value. I distrust that.

JS: How about political value?
MH: Ah, political value. Think about awareness, who we are, where we are. In *A Lover's Almanac*, Louise's aunt, who is a brilliant doctor, takes her out on a walk at the farm at night and cries out, "We are in it. The Milky Way, the Holocene"—it's the old micro/macro—so easy to forget our responsibility to our time.

JS: We forget that we are here now, in this place, at this time. The book is full of the number 2000, but this is not a futuristic novel, it is a novel about possibility. Perhaps this awareness you described opens us up to possibility. There's a passage in *Expensive Habits* where Margaret is thinking about the possible lives she didn't live. Maybe that's something fiction can do for us, wake us up to possibilities.
MH: But we don't live those other lives. It is a romantic idea, a turning away from reality, though perhaps a necessary fiction. It is awfully hard to be realistic about 1998, in America, in New York City, in this apartment. (*laughter*)

JS: Happy New Year, by the way.
MH: Yes, Happy New Year. (*pause*) Another thing I'm interested in is the glut of information that is available, which is much like the constant quoting and referencing that is in almanacs. We are awash with information. The *Science Times* on Tuesday . . . It's amazing, I love it. And yet it's too much to handle, the bottom of the sea, and the stars, and thus the collage forms.

JS: That's how I'd describe your last two books, as collages.

MH: Yes, but what can I make of it in a personal way? I don't want to be subjective, but how can one say that all this information sets some control on the randomness of daily life. Collage and weaving are ways of describing the process. But I was very taken by a video that my daughter gave me of David Hockney discussing his delight in Chinese scroll painting. You look at scrolls, and there are different stories along the line, as in a room full of tapestries. There is something going on in one corner and something going on in another corner; there are different scenes happening, and the eye travels from story to story to story. Yet we look upon one work of art.

JS: In another time you might have been called an experimental writer. I'm curious, do you set yourself in a group of writers, a group of peers whose ideas you share?

MH: Do they have to be contained to my generation? (*laughter*) Experiments I always say are for the lab. There have been certain periods where writing has been experimented with—automatic writing in the nineteenth century, the Dadaist games. But then if the experiment works, it's proven, it's no longer experiment.

On Writing *Make Believe*

Leonard Lopate / 2000

Joanna Scott talks with Leonard Lopate of *New York & Company*, WNYC, New York, February 9, 2000. Reprinted by permission of New York Public Radio (WNYC/WQXR).

Leonard Lopate: At first glance this book seems something of a detour from your usual themes. Not only is it set in the present, but it deals with some very au courant issues—race, adults battling for custody of children—not the sort of thing that we've seen from you in the past.

Joanna Scott: Yeah, I would like to say that I shift with each book. I don't know if it's a good thing or a bad thing, but I tend to turn my back on my last book. So, book by book, I think I'm not necessarily following any patterns. This seems in the way my next step, not necessarily a turning away from all my past work.

LL: And it deals with one of the greatest themes of American and American literature, race.

JS: Which I've dealt with before. I've written about slave ships and illegal slaving in the mid-nineteenth century. I've also worked race in in other ways. Because it's our country's concern, it's my concern as a writer.

LL: You once said that you weren't too good at writing about yourself, and that once you got started getting into history and other people's lives you were freed as a writer. But here you have moved a little closer to home. *Make Believe* is not your experience, but it's about your time.

JS: I was a little nervous about that. . . . I'd look at this wild world and I'd ask myself: How can I write about it? I don't know the words for things. I don't know the name of that person. I don't know his story. So it required more invention, and that's what I wanted to do. I wanted to push myself away from what had, in a sense, become a crutch for me, the crutch of history, the crutch of fact. I wanted to see if I could throw the crutch away for a book.

LL: And this very definitely relates to things that we've seen in newspaper stories recently, even though obviously you wrote the book before Elian Gonzalez's case came up. *Make Believe* is about a black boy and a white girl who fall in love, and he's shot and killed while she's pregnant with their child. His parents help her care for him. Her parents deny her, which is an atypical situation today. But soon she too is killed, and the grandparents fight over custody of the child. Even though he's never met his white grand-parents, the boy ends up with them—and that's a whole other matter here. You're not interested in the legal aspects of this. You don't even write about the court case except maybe the judge's literary tastes.

JS: I don't. I thought of that as a hinge. There are other hinges in the book too that are not visible, but they're crucial, they're essential. I try to explain why the judge makes that decision, a rational decision, but I didn't want to spend time writing a scene, a court scene, that I wasn't interested in. I was too interested in my characters to spend time in the courtroom.

LL: Do you think that this is likely to have happened—that a judge would have awarded a child to the parents who have rejected him rather than the ones who have been raising him?

JS: Well, I slipped in a little fact about how the white grandparents had been supporting the daughter financially. I also checked with some lawyer friends in my neck of the woods, and they gave me the nod. They felt it was okay given the idiosyncrasies of law.

LL: You have the white step-grandfather—it's not the boy's real grand-father—really being motivated by self-righteousness and a religious conviction. That's what compels him to take this child away from the grand-parents who've been bringing him up and who obviously adore him. So do you think that those are things—that religious conviction is something that would get somebody to do something so outrageous?

JS: Well, I want to say that anything I write about is a possibility. It's not nec-essarily a formula for the drift of religious thought. I think in this case that what you consider self-righteousness, it begins with confusion. The boy's step-grandfather wants to be a good man, and that becomes a fierce desire for him. And as it becomes fierce internally it needs some sort of external response.

LL: The way you structure the story is we meet these people and then we go back and we learn about them, much the same way as we experi-ence people in real life. You meet somebody, you don't know much about them, and then in time you learn more and more details. You've obviously chosen that approach for a reason, but it's one that we don't find in most novels.

JS: Tell me more about that. I'm not sure what is different here.

LL: It seems to me that what happens is that after you introduce the character you then go back and we learn about that character—in the same way that if I meet you. First I meet you in a very particular way and then I will eventually learn all these other things about you. So it allows you as a writer to go back and forth in time.

JS: Yes, structurally I'm kind of all over the place, aren't I? But it felt like fitting pieces of a puzzle together for me. It felt quite natural once I had a sense of how the structure would come together. The parts when I do go back in time, when I do elaborate on the lives of the people who are at that point of the narrative gone, it enabled me, yes, to tell their stories, to fill out the characters.

LL: But it also forces us to reassess our own sense of stereotypes and expectations.

JS: I see what you're saying. And then this hopefully is what happens every day with us as we sit here and talk.

LL: Things get more and more complicated.

JS: And a reappraisal goes on continuously.

LL: Is that something that happens while you're writing the book?

JS: Absolutely.

LL: You keep on throwing in complications?

JS: And it's part of the discovery of fiction that's so marvelous, that's so exciting. You have to work with the logic of a character. You break out of that logic and either you have to create another compelling logic that makes sense or you drift into a madness for the character. But usually you stay within that logic, that way of thinking. Within that way of thinking, you can do anything.

LL: And how much of the plot actually is known to you before you start?

JS: You want the truth here?

LL: Of course.

JS: Probably not a whole lot. I tend to . . .

LL: Because this is a novel with a big plot.

JS: It is.

LL: Usually plotted novels are thought out and then other things happen in the process.

JS: Yeah. I end up throwing out whatever I planned. I do plan, I really do. I plan all the way to the end and then I drop my plans. I change my plans. I alter them.

LL: The book forces you to consider what it's becoming.

JS: I'm constantly rewriting my outline as I'm writing along in my books.

LL: You also throw in another—well, I won't say confusing—but another thing that confounds us for a while. The characters have fantasies and nightmares and you present them as though they're the real thing. And then we figure out later that they're not necessarily. Bo even had a cat that isn't there. Other characters have things that we assume to be true and then discover are not true. That's part of the writing process?

JS: Yeah, since I'm so interested in consciousness—where does that take me?—that involves the edges of consciousness. And so those dreams, the conversations that don't take place but are imagined—they seem part of consciousness, part of the mind's work.

LL: And they lead to the title as well, *Make Believe*.

JS: Absolutely.

LL: You have often been linked with writers like Lydia Davis, as experimental authors. Do you think of yourself in that way?

JS: Well, in this regard, that is a journey into the unknown. Each book I write is something I'm trying out, it's a kind of proposition—will it work or not? I suppose you could call it an experiment. I would hope that, like Lydia Davis, like many other writers . . .

LL: Robert Coover, your teacher . . .

JS: He was my teacher. John Hawkes . . . Those writers like Hawkes or

Coover, Barthelme, are very different from one another. So the phrase tends to be used to lump together a wide variety of writers. And that's when I get a little nervous about the term.

LL: In this book, even though it's all written in the third person, you really adjust the third person so that we're in the minds of a lot of different people. We start off in the mind of a three-year-old. Obviously you can't write in the thoughts of a three-year-old—so the third-person strategy was the way to get around that?

JS: To a certain extent. I'd actually sat with my own young children and taken some notes and listened to the way their thoughts translated into language, if that makes sense. They would be thinking hard and the words coming out would be so wonderfully nonsensical, I guess—so free—and I couldn't quite use that language. Here and there I do. I try to evoke the wild language that a child has access to. But by using that narrator I can move in and out, and perhaps I describe a sensation that the child himself can't describe.

LL: Another powerful emotion is the protection of your two kids. You're the mother of two kids. Did the fact that you were raising these children affect your decision to pursue this kind of material?

JS: Yeah. The joy I feel with them, that is part of the impulse here that got me going. Their fascinating ways of looking at the world—I found myself imagining the world through their eyes, and so that helped me start to design a character, a child who is different from them. I had to make something new, something other. But certainly the fact is that they are my life and this is what I know best these days. Or this is what I want to know best, I should say—let me qualify that.

LL: Jayne Anne Phillips once said that she wrote a book, *Shelter*, out of fear for her boys because she felt so protective of them.

JS: That fear is great for any parent.

LL: "What would happen if I were dead and these kids were left to the power of the courts, other people?" Sometimes strange things happen. People we thought we knew well will act very oddly.

JS: Yeah, it's frightening. But I've learned how resilient children are and so tried to describe that.

Joanna Scott: An Interview by Bradford Morrow

Bradford Morrow / 2000

From *Conjunctions*, no. 34 (2000): 342–52. Reprinted by permission.

John Hawkes was the mutual friend, the mutual mentor, who wrote me extolling the virtues of Joanna Scott's first novel with that strange, beautiful title, *Fading, My Parmacheene Belle*. As usual, Hawkes was right, and the promise shown in *Fading* has been fulfilled with each new book. Over the years following that fond introduction, we've become friends, colleagues, comrades-in-literary-arms, and this interview—begun as an e-mail exchange—we completed over coffee in my apartment one late-winter morning this year.

Bradford Morrow: You have a gift for conjuring childhood consciousness, of depicting the many nuances of not-yet-knowing as it graduates toward knowledge. Tom, in *The Closest Possible Union*, and Bo, in your new book, *Make Believe*, strike me as completely realized children—not an easy triumph. We've known each other for a number of years, but I realize all I know about your childhood is that you grew up in Connecticut. Self-portrait of the artist as a young woman?

Joanna Scott: I've come to think that the freedom I had way back when was really formative. Maybe this is just a story I tell myself, useful nostalgia, but it seems to me in hindsight that the freedom I had as a kid was extraordinary. My three older brothers and I were all half wild. Our only responsibility was to return home unharmed at the end of the day. From a very early age I could go and do whatever I pleased. And what pleased me most was to roam the patches of fields and woods in our town and pretend to be someone else. That kind of play gave me both a connection to the world and the illusion of escape. When my adolescent sense of dignity kicked in, I had to look elsewhere for that paradoxical pleasure. Books started to fill the space of play. At the same time, I'd plant myself in front of the television and watch the string of afternoon shows—*Gilligan's Island, F Troop, The Brady Bunch, I Dream of Jeannie.*

Morrow: A personal favorite of mine. I wonder if that freedom to roam didn't somehow translate into the freedoms you naturally claim as a novelist—certainly your forms are fresh with each new novelistic journey you take. What books seized your interest when you began to read? Can you trace influences in any of those early authors you most liked?

Scott: From the blur of my childhood reading I remember best my love of Tolkien, Burnett, Lewis Carroll, Harper Lee. But the odd sources I kept returning to, the books that puzzled and enlightened, were a collection of old English tales, the *World Book Encyclopedia*, and a musty copy of the Bible—New Revised Standard Version. I admit that by the time I got to Revelation, I was really confused. But I wonder if together these books gave me a sense of literary form and its endless possibilities.

Morrow: Just as your television shows seem mostly set in an imaginary other world, this childhood reading list really expresses a love of wordplay and invented language—Tolkien, Lewis Carroll.

Scott: Invented places, too. I enjoyed the distance and differences, the excursions to other worlds. Then I read Faulkner: *The Sound and the Fury. Go Down, Moses.* I started writing what I dared to call fiction in response to Faulkner.

Morrow: What was it in Faulkner's work that struck sympathetic harmonics in you? I can see a shared Gothic temperament, an interest in darker resonances in the individual personality. Certainly, an embrace of language as character, if you will, of form as content. Your geographies are different. What were the affinities and what was it in an inchoate winter that made her want to take that immense leap from reader to writer, witness to practitioner?

Scott: It *is* immense, that leap. I'd like to say I had no choice—at some point in our lives the ground opens up beneath our feet. But the propulsion came from Faulkner and his ability to make the murky private work of consciousness meaningful. Faulkner persuaded me that even the strangest, most confused impressions deserve articulation. I read "The Bear" and heard for the first time the sound and beat of thought. Then there's the ending. That astonishing, wild ending. The squirrels in the gum tree. I wanted to write something that deserved such a finale. No surprise that I missed Faulkner's humor and could do no better than bloat my sentences with commas and adjectives and sincerity. Luckily, I was introduced to criticism fairly early on. My first significant experience was at a party. The father of a friend wandered into our midst, found my notebook on the table, and opened it to the first page of one of my earliest attempts at fiction. He started to read it aloud. Just a group of teenage kids and this Mr. So-and-So in a room listening to the silliest, most overwrought prose ever written. Line after line—what howlers! We were all in stitches. It was a long, portentous paragraph about a storm. Now it might seem this guy was being a little unfair, exposing me to ridicule that way. But I was happy to have my aspirations.

Morrow: You clearly survived this first encounter with criticism. Who were your earliest encouragers? I know that John Hawkes was an inspiration and a mentor.

Scott: In college, at Trinity and Barnard, I found my support in a few wonderful, idiosyncratic teachers, who helped steady me through those wobbly years. Later, at Brown University, I worked with Robert Coover—a famously tough, precise, passionate teacher—and I started to feel more at ease with the whole process of writing. He taught me how to use a computer (this dates me—I'm talking about life back in the Dark Ages), and once I learned the block-and-delete command I saw how liberating revision can be. Then John Hawkes returned after a year's leave. Jack was a hugely important teacher. He was a great comedian, a great writer, a devilish critic, a kind reader. He was—or pretended to be—endlessly perplexed. His complaints about a piece were cast as bafflement and comic misinterpretations. And yet I could hear the ring of truth in Jack's misreadings. With the last story I wrote for Jack's class, I tried something completely new. I gave up my attempts at elegance and created a narrator, an old fisherman, who begins, "I will tell you exactly how it was one day. . . ." And I meant it. That old man was going to tell it exactly how it was. But within a few words it became clear to me that his version depended upon his illusions, his bigotry, his habits and assumptions, and it took me many pages to explore this strange consciousness. When I was done with him I had my first novel.

Morrow: Your work is never evidently, plainly autobiographical—by which I mean to say that the old writers' workshop maxim, *Write only what you know*, seems somehow irrelevant, or at least shallow. Egon Schiele's life. The life of young Bo in *Make Believe*, whose mother was white and father black. The scientists and discoverers in *Various Antidotes.* The narrators of both *Fading, My Parmacheene Belle* and *The Closest Possible Union*. None of these relate in any easy way to Joanna Scott. What does this distancing mean for you as a writer? How do you research a boy such as Bo, his grandparents, his parents? What's the process?

Scott: I'm tempted to say that anything I ever write is no more than an accident. The fundamental mystery for me in any fiction is located in the confluence of circumstance and character, and when I start a fiction I can't know whether or not that confluence will be rich with mystery. I may have some plan in mind, but my plans usually don't see me through many pages. Especially with longer works of fiction, I experience a whole lot of false starts. I get to a certain point when I'm writing a novel and find that the elements aren't combining, mystery isn't being effectively generated, and I can't make the inflections of language work for me. So I start over. If I'm lucky, I stumble upon a subject that generates a novel's worth of wonder, and I keep going. I find that when the elements are strange to me, different and distant from my own life, the fictional concoction is more interesting. There's more to discover when I'm writing about an old fisherman, Egon Schiele, a small boy, a Coney Island witch, a Dutch lens grinder. Maybe when I'm eighty-five, I'll write my coming-of-age novel. But so far I've been able to invent more freely, and generate more mystery, by working with subjects that are, at least on the surface, unfamiliar. The research I do—if I dare to call it research—is haphazard, done at a glance, really. We take in so much at a glance. I glance at a stranger in a coffee shop and suddenly I feel I have an entire new novel in my head. Or I see a little pen-and-ink drawing or am struck by some piece of an anecdote. I have to say I've grown a little suspicious of research. Writers need to find various ways to gather information, but we use the word research to describe that process of gathering, and the next thing you know, authenticity becomes the highest value.

Morrow: And yet Bo's world strikes the reader as utterly "authentic." Its authenticity—verisimilitude, to use the painterly term—doesn't come into question during the experience of reading. Is this as much a function of the language used, then, prose itself, the form of the artifact, as it is of scenes and circumstances?

Scott: Think of Defoe calling *Robinson Crusoe* a just history of fact. Deception is a writer's great privilege. We use language to create a world, a feeling, a character, and we can call it true. We can lie. We can counterfeit.

Morrow: A novel's an authentic counterfeit.

Scott: Yes, and half the fun is in the pretense. We learn about the mind's astonishing powers of logic and invention as we read fiction—or write. I do want to make something genuine, but I get squeamish when authenticity is used in a prescriptive way to define some definite accordance with life. As long as it can describe both Vermeer and Braque, Dickens and Beckett, then it remains useful. This is the back-route answer to your question about language. These days I find myself most interested in the inflections of words. Old words, dull words, strange words—everything short of nonsense can be inflected in new ways. A distinct fictional consciousness is rendered by the slight elongations of meaning, the twisted, unexpected nuances. And it takes some sort of fictional event or circumstance to give an energy to the words, to make them spring into action.

Morrow: This calls to mind the taxidermic menagerie housed at the Manikin, and the library afloat in the Charles Beauchamp—in different ways manifestations of the power of obsession to bring imagination to life. Indeed, obsession seems to be a linking theme in many of the novels and stories.

Scott: It's true, I'm obsessed with obsession. Or maybe just mildly preoccupied. Or maybe it's a major linking theme for many of us, thanks in large part to Poe. We're imps of the perverse, we can't help it!

Morrow: Which leads me to ask you about the Gothic. Both of your most recent novels are informed, it seems to me, by an increasingly Gothic sensibility, an interest in how the imagination (of children, again) is shaped by encountering mortality—be it in the form of the classic Gothic manse with its suggestive imagery, or the violent death of a parent. How do you see classic Gothic theory and form influencing your work? Who besides Poe interests you? I could swear I've heard Charlotte Brontë humming behind some of your *Manikin* passages.

Scott: A wonderful thought, Charlotte humming—but not without her sisters. All those ghosts behind the cobwebs. And all that great new fiction you and Patrick McGrath gathered in your Gothic anthology. What is it that's so appealing about the form? It could be the possibility of giving weight to shadows. Raising the dead from their graves. But there's a simple explanation for my interest: I'm infatuated with the Gothic in its nineteenth-century manifestation—with Dickens, Emily and Charlotte Brontë (Emily more so, though you're right, I was thinking of Charlotte's Thornfield when I was building and furnishing my Manikin), Godwin at one cusp, Hardy at the other, and on this side of the ocean, Melville, Hawthorne and Poe (his weird, weird *Pym*). Sometimes I think that contemporary writers can best be described by their loyalties to either the eighteenth or nineteenth century. Some are Sternians, and others Dickensians. The Sternians are endlessly witty and aren't plagued by Dickensian sentimentality and melodrama. Sentimentality and melodrama—they produce great dreams and nightmares, unforgettable violence, madness, passionate love. But they also can look pretty silly on the page. Perhaps this is why nineteenth-century writers so often open their fiction with an apology, begging the reader's indulgence.

Morrow: What kind of reader are you? By which I mean to ask, when you're reading Melville or Dickens or one of the Brontë sisters, what is the experience—is it possible or even desirable to sideline the technician within who's there to glean formal ideas?

Scott: I'm reminded of Virginia Woolf's remark about reading George Eliot: "No one has ever known her as I know her." It's a wonderful feeling, a sense of privileged intimacy, that certain writers inspire. We have private conversations with people we've never met. But I don't do much talking back, at least not during the first encounter with a book. On a first reading I'm watching, listening, savoring the occasional shock of understanding, gliding down the page, sometimes drifting lazily. It's when I return to a book that I go with a pen in hand and try to decipher the method.

Morrow: Did you have the chance to visit the Nabokov centenary exhibit at the New York Public Library? I was mesmerized by his complex jotting, schema, and doodlings in his copies of Kafka, Joyce, and others. It was as if he read with his pencil, tattooing his way through the sentences, all but revisiting the compositional moment of scribing the words of his colleagues.

Scott: No, I missed that. I wonder if he'd have found Post-its useful. I do a lot with Post-its these days.

Morrow: Interestingly, Nabokov wrote often on index cards. So Post-its might have been right up his alley. If he tossed one up into a strong breeze and squinted, who knows but that it would've resembled a butterfly. Jane Austen wrote her novels on small sheets of paper. I remember seeing her manuscript of *Mansfield Park*, or *Emma*, at the British Museum—stacks of confiningly narrow fields of foolscap covered in her long, elegantly complex sentences. A paragraph might go on for pages. Everyone develops a composition method. Graham Greene's five hundred words written patiently each day. Kerouac's compressed writing binges. Marguerite Young developing her massive narratives over decades. What are your practices, rituals, your ways of working?

Scott: A wonderful catalogue of tricks and habits you describe. I like to sit by a window when I write, and I like to begin with pen and paper. The computer is a temptation, and sometimes I find myself starting a sentence on paper and finishing it on the screen. But I know I've had a good day of writing if my hand is smudged with ink from my pen. The method does change from book to book. I work hard to develop a sharper sense of what belongs and what doesn't belong as I move forward in a fiction. It has to do with voice, with the logic of character. The rules of a text are implied in the first sentence, and then they become more elaborately defined with the next sentence and the next. Even if I don't know as I'm writing precisely what rules I'm following, what the confines are, I have some sense of it, and that's what I try to honor in revision. I try to keep following the governing logic of a text. That means deciding what sort of observations and metaphors are available to my particular narrator. What words, what exclamations, are out of bounds? Does my narrator eat lobster thermidor or pancakes? Does a certain passage deserve a long unbroken block of full sentences or a short list of nouns? I need readers to help me do this. My husband, Jim Longenbach, is my first and best critic. We're constantly trading pages from our works-in-progress.

Morrow: Question at an oblique angle. Does the writer have social responsibilities in the work she produces, and outside that narrative textual work? I know you serve on the board of PEN, for instance. How do you see the writer's relationship with her community?

Scott: I'm discussing Chekhov's "Gooseberries" with my students later today—it's an illuminating illustration of this responsibility conundrum. In Chekhov's story, Ivan Ivanich tells his friends a story about his brother, who, late in life, is happy with his opinions and his gooseberries. The brother's example enrages Ivan Ivanich, who can't stand what he calls "a kind of universal hypnosis," and yet he considers himself too old to engage in the struggle, as he says. He has, at best, a passionate sympathy—or so he thinks. By framing this sympathy in a fiction, Chekhov keeps the problem sizzling, and readers can't help but consider their own silence and hypocrisy. The fiction is unsettling, like most great fiction. And it is ambiguity—a strange ambiguity—rather than polemics that makes it powerful. This is true for some of the great social realist writers of the nineteenth century—Dickens, Hugo, Tolstoy. *Les Misérables*, to take one example, is a truly strange novel, with the possessive, passionately sympathetic Jean Valjean at its center—a wonderfully mysterious center. But it's not enough to blend passionate sympathy and ambiguity. Anyone writing today has to be keenly aware of our potential for moral error. When a writer stands up and declares himself a witness, a spokesman for the masses, I get nervous. A writer must respond to "the terrible things in life," as Chekhov puts it. Usually, though, we can do no more than keep the problems visible, at least when we're inside the fiction. When we're outside, anything goes. Grace Paley's a good model—complex satire inside the fiction, passionate political activity outside the fiction.

Morrow: A section toward the end of *Make Believe* begins with the phrase, "Imagine yourself looking up from the bottom of Hadley Lake." And then, in *Various Antidotes*, the story "Nowhere" begins with a similar invitation, "Imagine a treeless landscape. . . ." The challenge to the reader is to imagine with you—what is imagination? How are we to imagine?

Scott: I've just been reading Elaine Scarry on this subject and my thoughts are in a bit of a flux about this. I find myself especially interested in the limits of the imagination. This is one of Scarry's subjects in *Dreaming by the Book*. And William Gass has that brilliant essay, "The Concept of Character in Fiction," in which he describes the way readers imagine a character. He points out that we can only imagine pieces of an image. When we're reading fiction our imaginative involvement is so piecemeal, so circumscribed. As readers we participate in someone else's dream. But there's something about the broken quality of that dream that makes fiction unique. A character in *Anna Karenina* enjoys the cold air against her bare shoulder. Tolstoy is directing us to consider this single sensation, to imagine Kitty's shoulder—only her shoulder. It's such an effective moment because it is limited. The most memorable images of fiction stand out because they are surrounded by darkness.

Morrow: Could we go through your novels and discuss the moment the idea for the book came into being? I've often found that the genesis moment, the personal circumstance, that prompts a narrative can sometimes have little to do directly with the novel's outcome.

Scott: Every novel I've written has been prompted by some sort of unexpected encounter. It often happens when I'm struggling with another piece of fiction. Often without even knowing, I'm looking, listening, waiting for the right accident.

Morrow: You're a place looking for an accident to happen.
Scott: Exactly! Which is what happened most recently with *Make Believe*, literally. A car overturned in the middle of the night outside our house. But the first novel, *Fading, My Parmacheene Belle*, originated in a story my husband told me about his grandmother. She was Pennsylvania Dutch, very neat and precise, and on the day she was going into the hospital for major surgery, she set out her husband's suit for him to wear to her funeral. That suit on the bed—it's an image with immense implications. In *Fading* I set out to explore those implications.

Morrow: Such as?
Scott: What would a man think as he stands alone in the bedroom staring at that suit? The single image became the prompt for the fiction. I imagined the tangle of emotions provoked by the image, and in the process of untangling the response, I started inventing a narrative voice.

Morrow: *The Closest Possible Union*?
Scott: I had begun a novel about a literary critic who wanted to exhume Ezra Pound's body in Venice and bring him back to the States, and I was in the library stacks looking for information on Pound's background. I was just browsing, really, and I came across a book about slave ships and slaving. I opened it to a random page and read an excerpt from a boy's journal. He describes watching an African man being hamstrung and thrown into the ocean. His voice was so peculiar—he was an incredibly observant and yet uncomprehending witness. I decided to mimic that voice in my own fiction.

Morrow: *Arrogance*?
Scott: I was at the fin-de-siecle Vienna exhibition at the Museum of Modern Art, and I heard some people laughing at one of Schiele's drawings, a self-portrait of the artist—a beautiful, grotesque sketch of the artist standing naked. The people were laughing, the man asking the woman beside him, "Would you buy a used car from this guy?" That's a powerful kind of laughter, isn't it? Arrogant laughter inspired by contempt, contempt inspired by indifference, indifference a defense against the artist's provocation. I went home and started reading about Schiele, and in my own arrogant fashion I decided I could write a novel about him.

Morrow: What I'm hearing here is that you reach a moment of personal availability to the coincidental, the happenstance, the unexpectedly pregnant moment, which has richer implications than might at first be apparent.
Scott: Right. We have to be ready to notice coincidence. Or else I'm just trying to give meaning to arbitrary experience. A few years back our neighbors put a stuffed deer out in their yard. A trophy from their last hunting trip. But I mistook the stuffed deer for a real deer. A beautiful white-tailed deer standing in the snow. I admired it through the kitchen window, I went outside and called to it, I picked up a snowball and threw it at the deer. And still it didn't move. I picked up another snowball, and threw it, and it hit the deer, and it still didn't do anything. That's when I realized I was dealing with an imitation. It turns out that my hometown of Rochester was a center for taxidermy at the turn of the century, and we still have some of the country's greatest taxidermists here. Taxidermy—it struck me as an irresistible metaphor. We kill life in order to create art. How could I not write a book about it?

Morrow: And *Make Believe* arose from a car accident?
Scott: A car overturned in front of our house in the middle of the night. I went out to help but couldn't get the doors opened, and the windows were tinted so I couldn't see inside. I thought for certain that the driver had been killed, since that side of the car had been flattened by the impact. It was a dark, damp night. The street was silent. The only sound was the car's blinker—tick tick tick. As it turned out, the driver, the only one in the car, had been thrown into the passenger seat and wasn't hurt. But I filled the car with my own story.

Morrow: There seems to be a common thread of filling something that had life in it before, but is missing its inhabitants. The eviscerated deer, the empty suit, the crashed car whose occupant has fled, even Schiele was not there to defend himself against the ridiculing laughter. And here's the artist, ready to fill those empty spaces with fresh life.
Scott: That's very intriguing. Maybe it's that whispering in the dark we do.

Morrow: What would you have done if you weren't a writer?
Scott: There was a time when I wanted to study rocks. There was a time I wanted to train animals.

Morrow: To do what?
Scott: To do whatever I wanted them to do, of course! And then there was a

time when I wanted to be a photographer. In high school I worked with an ambulance crew and I hung out at the local emergency room at night. I wanted to devote myself to medicine. And I wanted to sing in musical comedies.

Morrow: Who are your contemporaries with whom you feel an affinity?
Scott: Both as writer and editor, Brad, you've helped to tighten alliances among a pretty disparate group of writers. I feel grateful for that sense of connection to these extraordinary writers. And then there are the contemporary George Eliots—the strangers I know only through their work, writers I admire immensely. Calvino, García Márquez, Sebald, John Berger, Rushdie, Gordimer, Ozick, DeLillo, to name a few.

Morrow: Do you have a sense of what a Joanna Scott shelf should look like at the end of your writing life?
Scott: I want it to look just like this table here. With a shell, and a stone, and a little turtle, and a broken glass hand, and a dagger. And I just hope that when I'm all done—whether it's tomorrow, or in thirty years—that there's some coherence to it. I can't tell just now.

Joanna Scott

Martin Naparsteck / 2003

From *Lake Affect Magazine* 24 (2003). Reprinted by permission of Martin Naparsteck.

Rochester is my home, and my home is embedded in the details in my fiction, whether I'm writing about fin-de-siecle Vienna, the island of Elba in the 1950s, or Rochester's own Swillburg neighborhood in the 1990s. My initial plans for a narrative are inevitably bumped and changed by my daily experience. All it takes is a glance—a glance at a stranger in a coffee shop, a glance at an item in the newspaper—and when I return to my desk, I'll find my next sentence going in an unexpected direction. There's an improvisational quality to imaginative writing. It's a mix of foresight, insight, hindsight, and those odd thoughts prompted by the day's surprises.

I'm not the only writer who is hopelessly addicted to the physical action of arranging letters into words. At some level, I write because it's one important way of staying in motion and alive. But the compulsion begins with the diverse pleasures I've felt as a reader. Often these pleasures are unsettling. I'm especially grateful to those writers who explore the more unmanageable or inexplicable aspects of life, who in their portraits of fictional characters trace reason to the point where it begins to be shaken by uncertainty or to harden into fanaticism. The Brontës, Poe and Melville, Chekhov, Henry James, Woolf and Joyce, Faulkner, Beckett—I find their explorations of the mind amazingly suspenseful and illuminating. My writing begins with the amazement I feel as a reader.

My husband [poet James Longenbach] and I read each other's work backwards and forwards, through each revision. That I happen to have a partner who is so profoundly sensitive to the nuances of language and so elegant a writer—it's just my good luck, I guess. There are a couple of other friends with whom I share work in the early stages. And I've started to ask my children for advice.

Certain books—books I thought I knew well—have had an unexpected impact on me when I've gone back to them recently. James's *Portrait of a Lady*, Conrad's *The Secret Agent*, Woolf's *Mrs. Dalloway*, Mann's *Death in Venice*—all of these, along with many others, have been surprisingly disturbing. I guess part of my ongoing education as a reader has to do with learning to consider—and reconsider—the implications of a fiction.

I've been writing and publishing for almost twenty years, and I still find the invention of characters the most thrilling part of the process. I write to become someone else for a while. The prospect of being myself on the page seems less interesting. There is a certain amount of self-portraiture involved in the creation of fictional characters, just as daily experience helps determine the direction of a story. But it's the feeling of empathy, rather than the trick of disguise, that keeps me going.

We can write about anything and anyone. We can write about a man marooned on an island even if we've never been marooned on an island. We don't have to be experts in the field of microbiology to write through the point of view of a microbiologist. There's a tendency among contemporary writers to shore up their efforts with extensive research. We have to remember, though, that a work of fiction is not measured by its accumulation of facts. A novelist can master complex information and still write a terrible book. Or a novelist can write about a voice in a bottle and produce a masterpiece. There are some writers who move easily between intricate factual material and fiction, but they succeed because of the strength of the fiction, not the accuracy of the facts. While we expect to find some quality of illumination in strong imaginative literature, we usually don't read fiction in order to educate ourselves in a particular scientific or historical subject. Isn't the divergence from reality one of the most attractive aspects of fiction? It's wonderful that we never sufficiently grow up and never lose our love of make-believe. As long as we retain a passion for the unreal, we will continue to write and read fiction. Even if I could pretend to be an expert in myself (I'm not), my expertise wouldn't necessarily improve my fiction. I may borrow images or emotions from old memories and use knowledge I've accumulated from experience, but it really doesn't matter what autobiographical elements go into the mix; what matters is the coherence of the invented thing. Even if I begin with some reflection of myself, at a certain point I disappear into the character. That's what I mean by empathy. I lock logic, vision, and emotion, to a fictional sensibility. Of course, many writers succeed by using the premise of fiction to alter the real story they want to tell—the story of their lives. Writer X might become a bit more attractive as a fictional character than in person. Writer Y might use the fiction for confession. Writer Z might sneak in gossipy secrets. But a writer's colorful life story does not make a beautiful novel.

If I were afraid of making stupid mistakes, I wouldn't take the risk of writing. Nor would I gain much by faulting myself for mundane pleasures and appreciations. All those hours I spent watching TV as a kid. All those theme songs cluttering my brain. *Bewitched. Gilligan's Island. The Wonderful World of Disney.* Pop music. Sentimental docudramas. Steven King adaptations. It's fun being entertained. But it's more fun being enthralled. And since I don't have as much free time as I used to, I look for things that challenge and unsettle and enthrall me. I'm most interested in art that holds up to the sharper scrutiny of a second look. I learn by returning to something, rereading and reviewing.

Joanna Scott: Novelists

Ralph Black and Anne Panning / 2003

From SUNY-Brockport's Writers Forum with Ralph Black and Anne Panning on December 2, 2003, http://digitalcommons.brockport.edu/writers_videos/5/. Reprinted by permission.

(Editor's note: The interview begins with Joanna Scott reading a passage from her novel *Tourmaline*.)

Joanna Scott: Dad explaining that there are things a father can say only to his son, you telling Dad about an old episode of *Popeye*, Dad telling you something about the something he'd been wanting to explain, something having to do with the Nardi girl, you telling Dad about the time Popeye went overboard with his anchor, Dad warning you about the explosion of nothing into something, all you have to do is look at a girl for the fun of it, you reminding Dad about the BB gun you'd been promised, Dad reminding you that there are confidences a father can share with his son, his wife never needs to know, no one else needs to know what the father says to his son on this balmy moonlit night on the island of Elba after too many days of rain, you telling Dad you were kind of tired, asking, "Can't we go home now and if we can't go home, do you want to play ants?" Dad asking, "Why the hell did we come here anyway?" but you weren't sure whether he was asking why did we come here to this place in the woods or to this island, Dad pointing out that we could have gone to Mexico or Alaska or Louisiana while you tried not to yawn and to keep yourself awake you decided to explain what a periscope is, Dad cursing his Averil uncles, you reminding Dad that your birthday was in 10 and a half months, Dad reminding you that you were an innocent child, you telling Dad that, unlike your brothers, you don't actually fall asleep, you just lie in bed thinking about sleep, Dad saying that even if you didn't understand what he was saying, it sure felt good to talk, what a relief just to talk, father and son, you unable to suppress a great big yawn, Dad giving a sad chuckle of resignation and cuddling you against his chest, you hearing his laugh as a crackle echoing from the cave of his ribs, Dad shifting you a little so he could free his arm, rubbing his face as if he had a towel in his hands and you were blotting his wet skin dry, you lying there thinking about sleep, Dad saying, "If only," you telling Dad you were cold, though you weren't cold at all, you just wanted him to put his arm around you again, Dad saying that what he'd like right then was a scotch, you thinking lazily about blowing the fluffy parachutes from the head of a dandelion, Dad repeating, "if only," you enjoying the vibrations of his voice against your ear, Dad telling himself, "if only he hadn't come to Elba," getting only this far in the hypothetical, Elba being the place where his troubles began as far as he could see, and he couldn't see very far, not in the dark, not with his son asleep across his chest, not with his head aching as the evening's alcohol dissolved, not with regret fogging his vision, regret an effective cover for the terror of self-knowledge, the story he could tell himself the story of an American guy who fucked up, don't we all fuck up sooner or later, he's sorry, Claire, he's sorry, Adriana, his deception, her deception, his cowardice, Francis Cape, all of which kept him from considering his original purpose in leaving home and thus he was able to make the decision to feel nothing worse than guilt, which manifested itself visibly with the hint of a smirk, a smirk which would never entirely disappear from his face, marking him as the kind of person who, with a shrug, was always ready to acknowledge his potential for fucking up, no matter what he did, he kept fucking up, sorry about that, Girls, regret lit with a soft glow of virility, that radiant Y chromosome, that sexy ex, the story such people could tell, always the same story, Sir Winston who loved Lady Jane who loved the Duke who loved Lady Jane's sister who loved Sir Winston, never more than that, never less, you know the kind of people I'm talking about, the edge of their personality a little dulled, their eyes a little blank, ambition a little muted, and always that smirk to signal to others that they'll never be registered saints, and guess what, they don't give a damn, let someone else rise to the challenge, they can have it along with all the trouble, the confusion, the uncertainty, the suffering, the intensity of thought and feeling, no thanks, Malcolm Murdoch is going to ease himself into sleep by thinking about the only thing that really matters to a man who hasn't eaten for 24 hours, the antidote of food, in particular, a bloody steak just off the grill, green bean casserole, and well in a mountain of mashed potatoes filled with steaming gravy.

Ralph Black: Welcome to the Brockport Writers Forum, a continuing series of conversations with contemporary writers. I'm Ralph Black, codirector of the forum, joined today by my colleague and codirector, Anne Panning and

our guest, novelist and fiction writer, Joanna Scott. Joanna is a professor of English at the University of Rochester and the author of many books including *The Manikin*, which was a finalist for the Pulitzer Prize in 1997 and *Arrogance*, a finalist for the PEN/Faulkner Award. Her collection of short stories, *Various Antidotes*, also a finalist for the PEN/Faulkner, won the Southern Review Short Story Fiction Award in 1995. She's been awarded fellowships from the Lannan and Guggenheim Foundations and was given a fellowship from the MacArthur Foundation, their so-called Genius Award, in 1992. Her most recent novel, *Tourmaline*, came out to wide acclaim last year. Joanna, welcome.
Scott: Thank you.

Black: A great pleasure to have you here slogging through an early Rochester snow storm to get here.
Scott: We're all used to it.

Black: Yeah, we are all used to it. I know that Anne and I have some questions about *Tourmaline* and maybe particularly about the passage that you just read, but maybe we can start by having you talk a little bit about your life and where you came from, and particularly I'm interested in where the urge to tell stories came from.
Scott: Okay.

Black: For you.
Scott: My life's not that exciting. I was raised in a suburb in Connecticut and stayed there until I was eighteen and then went off. But now that I watch my own young children, I've been thinking about how I was able to spend long hours playing outside. I'm not sure we make time or allow time for our children to play freely. Most of my memories of childhood begin with knocking on my friend's doors and asking if they could come out and play. I was convinced that no one else ever had quite as much time as I did to play. I had a seemingly infinite amount of time to play, all day long. By the age of five or six, I was just out of the house wandering around the neighborhood. I learned to play on my own to some extent. I kept trying to draw my friends out of their houses and organized them into these games of make believe. Even when they didn't want to, I would try hard to get them out there. I wonder if I exhausted them with my determination to just keep playing.

Black: You will play now.
Scott: It's like Miss Havisham calling out in *Great Expectations*, "Play! I

want to watch you play!" At a certain age it became clear that I was getting too old to play. And that was the age when I started to pick up my pen and make scratches on paper and somewhat in secret, taking my imaginative life elsewhere into language.

Black: What were the early scratches like? Were they narrative story scratches or poems?

Scott: There was a transition stage. When I started to feel a little too mature to be wandering around the neighborhood pretending I was a revolutionary soldier, I started to make little figures out of Play-Doh, and I'd arrange them in a kind of diorama in a shoe box. That shoe box became the place where I could act out my stories. When I was twelve, we moved across town to another house, and I thought hard about it, and I hid that box full of Play-Doh figures in the back of the closet, and I left it there in the old house. I did not take it with me because I was too embarrassed at that point. But it filled an important need for me, allowing me to keep making up stories. I'm reminded of J. M. Coetzee's fascinating essay about play and the somewhat restrictive roles that we come to rely on when we play established games, rather than imaginative games. He points out that we should be allowed to make up our rules more often. When I moved to the new house and hit adolescence, I looked around for a new form of play. I started to write a little, usually fragments of stories. Later I tried poetry in school, but my first attempts were prose, half-written stories that often didn't get finished. I seemed capable of generating lots of ideas. I liked to start stories but not end them. I grew impatient and was eager to move on to something else. But there was a narrative drive right from the start. I think it made sense that I was living these stories, first in person in the woods and fields around my house, and then with these little clay figures, and then with words.

Black: It's funny, this image of a little girl and the clay figures particularly in the box and hiding them away. It sounds like a character in any number of your books. I can imagine her in *The Manikin* certainly. The Revolutionary War image strikes me because so much of your work is interested in history, particularly the history of science. Where did that passion and interest come from?

Scott: Let's see. My first book involved an old fisherman who exists in a contemporary world that he doesn't recognize. He feels that he belongs to another period of history and the contemporary world is grotesque to him.

To the world, however, he's the one who's grotesque. To imagine an interior life for this character, I had to do some research, that took me into unfamiliar areas. I started to read journals and letters from the nineteenth century, even though, as I said, he is a contemporary character. It was at that point, as I was beginning my first novel, when I started to realize the benefits of gathering information. I used to call it research. Now I prefer to call it gathering. By my second book, I was quite bold about that and felt I could use a voice that was archaic, set in another time on an illegal slave ship in the mid-nineteenth century. I read as much as I could about the period. I read secondary sources, including a journal by a young white boy. I never could verify the authenticity of that source. But authenticity didn't matter to me at the time. I was interested in the way perceptions were described. I spent a lot of time in the dusty stacks of our university library. I became excited about the possibilities hidden on the shelves, the secrets inside books that hadn't been taken out for fifty years, the stories that have been lost and forgotten. Why I was interested in history, I don't know. Maybe it goes back to those days of playing. The thing I most liked to imagine was the period in the eighteenth century in my hometown in Connecticut. I guess I was revved up by a couple of books I'd read about the era.

Anne Panning: Were your parents and siblings big readers? Was it that kind of family where you were you a bookish kid?
Scott: No. They were big on football. Football was the thing. And I loved football too. I would put on my helmet and go running into the neighborhood, looking for friends to join me on a team. We didn't have many books in the house. There was a lot of talk in my family about reading. I think some members of my family might object if they heard me say we weren't big on reading because, in some ways, we all thought of ourselves as a bookish family. But we spent most of our time outside.

Panning: I'm wondering how you got from there to the part where you got fascinated by research and history. What was your formal training as a writer? Did you go through the normal process of getting an MFA and studying creative writing?
Scott: I did. Although, back then it wasn't really a normal pursuit. I found myself in New York after graduating from college, working at a literary agency during the day and trying to write when I got home. I would get off the subway and go straight up to my apartment on the corner of 111th Street, and I would sit down at my typewriter. I saved up my first salary

checks to buy a big pink refurbished IBM typewriter. I lugged it uptown, and I put it on my desk and rattled away. I was one floor above Broadway, and the room would be so noisy, full of the sounds of the city coming through the open window, along with the sound of my typing. It was frustrating knowing that I had to get up for work at seven the next morning. I didn't have the time I wanted and needed. I was trying out a lot of new things and failing at a lot of new things. I didn't have enough time to fail. I needed more time to throw out work. That's when I decided to go back to school. I'd heard about people going to something called an MFA program. I wasn't really sure whether I wanted to apply to a PhD program in literature, which seemed more practical, or to go to an MFA program. I ended up applying to MFA programs and went to Brown University, where I worked with some interesting people. First, Robert Coover and then Susan Sontag and then Jack Hawkes. While I was working with Jack, I wrote a story that became the first chapter of my first novel.

Black: The trajectory of your work is interesting. This may be a cliché, but a lot of young writers start by writing short stories, and then, after publishing a collection or two of short stories, they start working toward the novel. But you went the other way. You started with the story, developed it into a novel, and then published two or three novels.

Panning: To add to that, many writers start with an autobiographical novel. The thing that is your story, and then you go from there. Your trajectory is completely unlike that.

Scott: My first novel is narrated by an old fisherman who has lost his wife after fifty-three years. But it's really an autobiographical novel.

Black: The old saying that you write what you know—you, by contrast, are writing what you gathered.

Scott: I was thinking about this the other day. Why do we say to fiction writers, "Write what you know?" We don't say that to musicians. We don't say that to artists. "Paint what you know." We don't insist on that. Why do we do that with fiction writers? Sometimes it seems to me that our sense of realism is more constrained today, and the rules governing novels are stricter than they were in the nineteenth century. We think of Dickens as a realist, but when you really dig into his novels and consider the intense eccentricities of his characters and the often stylized, theatrical speech, it's hard to make a case for the fiction as realistic.

Panning: It's something about the authenticity. We had a story in my 300-level workshop today about an Aztec mask that somebody found, and it was great. We suddenly all sat up because it wasn't the usual what you know. We didn't know. She didn't know. The research adds a lot.

Scott: I think people have started to grow tired of hearing, "Write what you know." It's still said and will probably not be said for much longer. Unless the docudrama triumphs and we lose fiction entirely. Which is a possibility. You know, *based* on a true story will no longer need the word "based." Everything told will be a true story.

Panning: Your stories are really funky. I'm really drawn to the book. It's so different from most short fiction that you read. But I was wondering in terms of the obvious time of labor and so on of writing a novel how you proceed, what your practice is in terms of going after a short story, writing a short story versus a novel, in terms of what you want to accomplish in each. There's the epiphany story and all of this, but yours don't really seem that traditional.

Scott: I've been reading a lot of the work of Lydia Davis lately, and I'm so struck by how every single thing she writes takes a different form. That form may be a sentence long or it may be thirty pages long, it may be a dialogue, or it may be a single paragraph. I didn't know there were so many available forms. I'm reminded how important structure is to fiction. And in terms of my concern with structure, I think for me the stories aren't that different from the novels. I'm always trying to find the form that's integral to the subject. I will do that in the novel. I will do that in the stories. The stories have different forms. I'm particularly comfortable with the fragmented form, in varying constructions. But I have to contain the story in a way that I don't have to contain the novel. I have to end my stories. And that takes the kind of discipline that I don't necessarily have [laughing].

Panning: But you were talking before about your method. You said you have a method. You've sort of developed this method as you started your first novel that kind of works for the other books you've done.

Scott: Although, I have to say that once I've published a book, I'm done with whatever method I used to write it. I couldn't simply go to the library and gather material and write the same book over and over, drawing in the same way from history. I couldn't do it. I refuse to keep writing the same book.

Panning: So, how does it change?
Scott: I try to come up with new methods.

Panning: How does it always change?
Scott: With my first collection of stories, I told myself, "I'm not going to rely on these historical figures in the way I did with *Arrogance*," and I'm not going to make the same use of historical documents as I did with my second novel, *The Closest Possible Union*. I tried to bring in more imaginative material in *Various Antidotes*, to mix with the history. With *The Manikin*, I drew from some historical sources, but just a little, without saturating myself. And then I decided to just turn back to the contemporary world with *Make Believe*. For that book, I had to go down to the neighborhood garage and learn what I could about car engines. And so with each book I have found myself gathering in a different way. And I had become increasingly nervous about research as a necessary step. Just as I don't want to tell my students, "Write what you know," I don't want to say, "Do your research," either. Writers need to find a unique method for each book, just like we find the form that is integral to the subject. Both method and form should keep changing, I think.

Black: In relation to *The Manikin* and *Tourmaline*, a couple images pop into my mind, images of puppeteers where you are taking these characters and you are setting them on a particular stage and just letting them spin and seeing where their lives on the stage will lead them. The research is there if you're going to talk about the chemical composition of tourmaline, but you have to do that work and get it right. Otherwise, the geologists who are reading your book are going to be jumping all over you.
Scott: I know. That's why I consulted with a geologist. And I thought, "Oh, I wish I'd gone into that field." Forget the fiction! I want to study rocks.

Black: It wears, I think, very lightly. It's kind of wonderfully integrated. It's like Eliot's famous dictum about form being no more than an extension of content. Do you see that as a method for yourself?
Scott: Yes. There's an accidental quality to it for me. I put my hands in this bag full of stuff and then, if I'm lucky, I find the form I need. But I don't always. I might think I have a fine idea and I can't find the form that matches the subject.

Black: So, how in *Tourmaline* did you find the form of this conversation between Oliver and Claire?

Scott: I had an idea of the progression of the narrative told solely from Oliver's point of view. But after I finished his first full chapter, I wanted to keep him thinking about what he didn't know, which is hard to do if you're telling a story based on accumulated knowledge. It's hard for us to remind ourselves of what we don't know. So I drew in Claire's voice to interrupt and correct. "That's not how it was," she said, "let me tell you how it was." That dialogue between the two provided me with something that fed my imagination. It seemed to lock the ongoing story into place, and I could move on. It helped to have a beautiful island off the coast of Tuscany to explore. First I imagined it from afar, but I also had to do my proper gathering and go to Elba and climb around.

Black: And you are heading there again for more gathering?
Scott: Yes. Yes. At the center of *Tourmaline* there's a very short retrospective scene about the war, the liberation of Elba. I couldn't tell the story of the liberation in the way I wanted to tell it. After I finished *Tourmaline*, I decided I wasn't done with that particular subject, and I needed to go back to it. I've been exploring and trying out some fictional approaches to the subject, trying to write about this violent period in the history of this island.

Black: In my writing classes, sometimes I'll use the image of the geode for students. Sometimes you find an image or a line in a poem that is geode-like, and if you crack it open, there might be all kinds of wonderful discoveries to be made there.
Scott: And it's often ugly on the outside, just gray and plain.

Black: I get that sense from this new project that the image of Adriana in the cabinet becomes a geode to free and open another cabinet of wonders.
Scott: Yes. But it does remind us of the accidental quality of all imaginative writing. Doesn't it? I mean, do you feel this? Sometimes you get an idea from a conversation you have in the grocery store, or you end up writing a book because of something that happened when your car broke down. These accidents or interruptions in our lives, the experiences that intrude upon our routines, they are the stuff that can spark art.

Panning: As we've been talking, I was thinking that setting is really primary for you: the taxidermy mansion in *The Manikin* or especially *Tourmaline*. To me, setting is where things start. But I want to turn to craft and technique for a second. I know that writers don't really think about them separately, but can you talk about whether you have something like setting or something life craft as the conscious priority when you write?

Scott: Can you give me an example?

Panning: For me it would be setting. I start with setting, and that's usually where everything starts from and centers around.

Scott: And how do you come up with those settings?

Panning: You are sitting at a rest stop somewhere on I-90 or you remember something or through travel. You know, all of it.

Scott: For me there's a kind of theatrical element to setting. In fact, sometimes I think I would have preferred to have been a playwright. I did write one play. It was great fun, but when I experienced it in production, it was terrifying to me. Never again! No, I might do it again. It was so exciting.

Panning: Well, it's like writing with your hands behind your back in a way because you are so limited. I think the fiction writer writing a play is incredibly hard.

Scott: What I didn't expect was how profoundly different the words become when the audience enters the theatre. You can see the play in dress rehearsal, all finished, ready to go, and then the audience comes in and it's a totally different piece of work. But it's illuminating, helpful to experience that. So in imagining settings for fiction, I think of them with a slightly theatrical or artificial quality. And I don't mean that I ever want to miss the chance to describe what it means to be in a real setting, what it means to experience the complexity of sensual perception. I want to capture that in language. But it's like that little box, that shoe box with the Play-Doh figures. You know? I'm aware of placing words to create the diorama.

Black: Place is so important. Wendell Berry has this great line where he says that we can't know who we are until we know where we are. That relationship between identity and place is so important for him. When I think about *Tourmaline*, I think about how Murray and the boys respond to place. It couldn't be more divergent. They are out there wandering the same mountains looking for their treasures in a way. Murray walks up to the cave and sits down and has a smoke and takes a nap and walks away. But the boys find wonder after wonder. That sense of the uncanny, that the world is imbued with life. There is that wonderful moment when they find the star in

the steel tube or something. And then they toss it aside. They say, "Okay. It's great for a few minutes," and then they are off again.
Scott: Experiencing magic.

Black: Yes. Exactly. So that is the kind of theatricality where place becomes a sort of backdrop for character.
Scott: Yes, and if it is successful, it has to have some deep connection to character. For me, that's where my fiction begins, or what excites me most, what we've come to call character. And when I was in graduate school, I remember reading Robbe-Grillet—psychology had become an immature subject, and we were supposed to move past it. There is definitely room to be skeptical of the simplistic cause-and-effect psychology that diminishes the intricacy of behavior. But we can't give up on psychology. My teacher Jack Hawkes famously railed against the notion that we create characters out of words. Actually, you can tell from his fiction that he loved creating characters. Even Beckett doesn't give up character. Some writers prefer to emphasize voice. It doesn't have to be a singular voice associated with a character, as Beckett shows us. But I still like that word *character*. It has a nice crunchy sound, doesn't it? And I'll argue that setting grows out of character. I'm trying to think, do I ever have a setting that isn't inflected in some way by the character, or by a very idiosyncratic narrator who's describing it? I don't think I do. Setting is described through impression. I want the physical world to be felt. I want to emphasize again and again what it feels like to be in the world, what it feels like to walk over a mound of earth, to travel over varied terrain, to experience the weather. Charles Wright endlessly contemplates the weather in his poetry. I feel that I could read about the weather for weeks and weeks. I could spend my life reading about nothing else but the weather. The weather is so interesting. How do we give a sense, through language, of what it really means to be in snow or rain or to feel the humidity around us? I'm always trying to do that through a singular sensibility—through a character's impressions.

Panning: So, was that what you were referring to when you talk about Robbe-Grillet and so on with the character statement that you said?
Scott: Well, I couldn't give up psychology. I couldn't give up character. I couldn't lose the interior of the human psyche in fiction. In fact, if anything, I've gone further into subjectivity. It is a particular subjectivity that I create in fiction.

Panning: Having studied with Robert Coover, I'm thinking of your graduate school experience. Do you think he had an influence on you and do you think he would call your work experimental?

Scott: You know what Robert Coover did? He taught me how to use a computer. I came to graduate school with my big IBM pink typewriter, and he said I had to learn how to use a word processing program. And I was too impatient to learn on my own, so he took the time to sit down and teach me this new computer program called Script. That was before Bill Gates got his hands on everything. That is emblematic of the way Bob Coover interacted with his students. He was very exact. Reading our work, he would make us think hard about a single word in a sentence. He'd want to know why we used that word. He'd make lots of marks on our stories—he took a lot of time reading our work. He was very helpful and a good model for me as I went on to be a teacher myself.

Panning: Would you call your work experimental? Or when people call your work that, what do you think? Do you think that fits you? Does that fit with what you think of yourself as a writer?

Scott: Yes. I would hope that all art is experimental to some degree. But perhaps it's a word that's thrown around too easily. I get most excited about work in any genre that makes me think of new possibilities. And it can do it in the quietest, most subtle way. It doesn't have to be in-your-face new and different. It can be Chekhov.

Panning: You talked about the novel *Everything Is Illuminated* at the reading a couple weeks ago, which could be described as experimental. It takes chances, that's the thing.

Scott: Absolutely.

Panning: Are there other works that you've read recently like that?

Scott: A writer I have just come to adore is Sebald. The book *Austerlitz*, in particular, I found just utterly satisfying. So moving. It is the story of a man's quest to recover his lost past, and his story is wrapped in the strange narrator's impressions. This narrator keeps fading in and out of the text, serving as a connection between the reader and Austerlitz. Sebald's doing fascinating things using images, taking the narrative in really unexpected ways. It is tempting to think of the associative quality of his narratives as somewhat arbitrary. But he's so in control. And his work never seems ostentatiously experimental. It's just unique, a unique sensibility expressing itself through a profound control of language. Of course, it's coming through translation, so we have to thank his translator, too.

Black: Do you find that there are writers like Sebald whose work you return to, whose work sort of feeds you as a writer?

Scott: Yes. Just the other day, I slapped on my desk *The Magic Mountain* and *Absalom, Absalom!* I don't know why. I just put those two books on my desk so I could crack them open and get the sound of the language in my head. In my early years as a writer, I liked to begin the day with Faulkner and get the sound of his language in my head—it helped me to face the blank page each day. But now—I mentioned Chekhov earlier. I go back and back again to Chekhov. There's a quietness there that I admire. Again, I'm speaking of the English translation. I mean, it's frustrating to think that there's even more to his work that I can't absorb. But I love the way the grotesque is contained in a quiet prose. And there's extraordinary compassion in his representations of solitude and loneliness and miscommunication. There's intense violence. It's quite extraordinary. So, he's been a writer I've gone back to. I go back to Virginia Woolf to think about the way a sentence can move, the way a narrative can move through time.

Black: Mentioning Woolf, Faulkner, and Mann, but Woolf and Faulkner particularly, as some kind of influence. And, back again to what you read at the beginning. It's just this kind of wonderfully lyrical meditation where the rhythms of the language propel that sentence, as they oftentimes do in those wonderful sentences by Woolf or by Faulkner.

Scott: Once I can create a character who exists within the confines of something we call a self, then I can start to shape it, to design this linguistic pattern that has, hopefully, some driving rhythm that tells me how to place the emphases, the beats in sentences that follow.

Panning: So, that's certainly a departure from the traditional, straight narrative. In a way that is as bold as in some parts of *Ulysses* or something. It seems to borrow from modernist writing.

Scott: Sure. I'll be as bold as Joyce. I have nothing to lose. Right? No, I think in terms of sound, I learn from Dickens. For rhythm, I look to Dickens. For the wildness of language, I look to Faulkner. But when it comes to repetition and rhythm, no one does it better than Dickens. And to great comic effect, which I've yet to master. And he can position words so that the repetitions keep varying. Hemingway must have learned it from Dickens.

Black: I know this was kind of a joke earlier on, but you don't actually worry about the death of the novel?

Scott: All the time. I find myself, in more peevish moods, wondering why people are so afraid of the imagination. This need to create authentic texts to have real-life situations on television, to have based-on-a-true-story narratives in the cinema—it just frustrates me sometimes that we don't value play. That we can't see the value of the mind's imaginative work. But that's been a problem facing novelists for hundreds of years. I love sending my students back to Defoe to see his argument in *Robinson Crusoe*. Crusoe's story is supposedly truer than life, than history. The fictional story is more authentic . . . somehow it tells us more. It treats its subject with more care, even as it tries to outdo history. It's a game, a contest, a competition between history and fiction—it's been going on since the genre of the novel has been flourishing, in English, at least.

Black: Thoreau thought that Melville was wasting his time as a writer because he was writing fiction. You know? He thought, if you're going to write, tell the truth.

Scott: Melville wondered that too. You feel him wondering that in *Moby Dick*. You're right. There will always be an ongoing concern about the superfluous nature of fiction, or the frivolous nature of fiction. We are not going to shake off the worry that the unrealities of fiction make it inconsequential. It's always going to be there.

Panning: So, would it be fair to say that you have no interest in writing memoir?

Scott: I wouldn't say no to any possibility, so we'll see.

Panning: How about short stories? Are you still writing those alongside your novels or do those just come randomly?

Scott: They are usually between novels. They're what I work on when I've finished a longer project. But now I'm going back and forth a little bit more than I have in the past because I have an idea for a continuous series of stories. But I'm not sure if that's going to come to anything. Time is just so scarce these days. I usually focus on one project.

Black: Let me ask you this. We've been talking a lot about rhythm and sentences. Can you take us out, as they say, by reading the opening of *Tourmaline*?

Scott: Oh, sure.

Black: Just the opening passage.

Scott: Water laps against the quay of Portoferraio. Hungry dogs blink in the sunlight. A grocer stacks oranges. A carabiniere checks the time on his wristwatch. A girl chases a cat into a courtyard. Men argue in the shade of an archway. A woman rubs a rag over a shop window. Heels click on stone. Bottles rattle in the back of a flatbed truck. A boy writes graffiti on the wall above the steps leading to the Liceo Raffaello. German tourists hesitate before filing into a bar. An old woman, puzzled to find herself still alive at the end of the century, sits on a bench in Piazza Repubblica, her eyes closed, her lips moving in a silent prayer to San Niccolo.

With Joanna Scott:
Author of Six Novels

Carole Burns / 2004

I discovered Joanna Scott when I read one of her stories in the *Paris Review*. It was as intricate and complex as a novel, yet as clear as a stone in water.

Immediately I went to find more of her work: first her story collection, *Various Antidotes*, then her novels. She takes on science and the natural world, both expansively and in miniature. In the opening of *The Manikin*, a single owl comes to realize it must fly south early this year. In this moment, Scott traces the mystery of instinct.

By now, she has published six novels and been awarded a MacArthur grant.

Scott was online Thursday, March 11, at 1:00 p.m. ET to talk about her work. A transcript follows.

Host Carole Burns is a fiction writer with short stories published or upcoming in *Washingtonian Magazine* and several literary journals. Twice a fellow at the MacDowell Colony, she's at work on a novel.

Editor's Note: Washingtonpost.com moderators retain editorial control over Live Online discussions and choose the most relevant questions for guests and hosts; guests and hosts can decline to answer questions.

Carole Burns: Hello, book lovers, and welcome to *Off the Page*. We have Joanna Scott with us today from Italy, and we're ready to get to the first question.

Harrisburg, PA: Do you have many ideas for novels? How do you narrow your ideas down into the novel you choose?

Joanna Scott: So far in my years as a writer, I have had a lot of ideas and a lot of dead ends. So I find myself writing in one direction and then another, and sometimes it clicks, and sometimes it doesn't. I feel there has to be a certain amount of improvisation as I'm writing, which means any idea or any commitment to a project is risky. It involves time, it involves gathering material, and sometimes it just doesn't work. Sometimes it does. As I'm starting out on a project, I can't tell if it will click or not. If it will keep generating its own future, in a sense.

It partly has to do with the independence of the characters, the strength of the voice. If I feel there's a distinct voice that deserves to keep speaking, that has a music of its own, a rhythm of its own, then I find myself seduced by the voice that I've created, but that I feel that I'm hearing from elsewhere.

There's a point I set for myself, and it's an arbitrary point, when I think no matter what happens I'm going to finish that book. And that's when I get to page 100. I have to see it out.

There are two points of exhilaration for me, when I'm writing. There's the point of reaching page 100, when I think, I've got something here. And then there's the point when I write the final word, and I say, Okay, that's done.

Although I once heard William Gaddis say he wrote long books because he didn't like them to end. And I can understand that.

Burns: Why do you suppose you turn so often to the past for your novels? What is it that the past tells us—or that so intrigues you?

Scott: Partly it's different. It requires discovery. So I go to the past to learn something. Partly I think I like to imagine a fictional reality for an actual reality that's been lost. Just like I try to give voices to characters who can no longer speak, I try to animate something that existed at one point. In a sense, I'm trying to animate the dead. I can't do that, so I move into the fables, the make believe of fiction, where we all know, readers and writers, that the ghosts are inventions. But it's a wonderful pretense.

Telling ourselves that fiction is in a sense true and at the same time not true is essential to the art of fiction. It's been at the heart of fiction from the start. Fiction offers truth, and we know it's a flat-out lie. Sometimes it drives a novelist mad. Sometimes it energizes us. Sometimes it's a mathematical problem we have to deal with, the truth and the falsehood of fiction.

I love seeing in novels a declaration of truth. We need to think about the action of interpretation when a writer who is lying tells us he is telling the truth. But it's an exciting stance, for both readers and writers. And it becomes more complex as we grow older and become more mature readers.

I feel as a writer, I'm addressing this in each book a little bit more precisely or deeply or obsessively. The relationship between the truth and the falsehood of fiction is something I keep wanting to write about in my work.

Bethesda, MD: How many books did you write before publishing your first? Did you ever consider yourself primarily a short story writer?
Scott: Oh, maybe twenty or thirty.

More seriously, I kept trying to write a book, and tried and tried and tried, and did, and that was my first book. But I didn't finish an entire manuscript with those early attempts. It's a learning process to write a novel and then put it away, and move on to more mature work. For better or worse, the first novel I wrote was published.

Long ago, I actually thought I might be a poet. Then I changed my mind, and I started to work on stories, through college, through graduate school. I worked hard, felt dissatisfied with the work I was doing, and finally I began a story with the line, "I will tell you how it was." And that became the first line of my first novel. Somehow that insistence that I was just going to tell you, no matter what, made the imaginative possibilities of fiction suddenly available to me. But that meant that before I knew it, I was no longer a short story writer, I was a novelist.

But I still write stories, and I try to create many different forms. I've tried to write for the theater, I still try to write poetry, I write in short forms and long forms.

Gullsgate, MN: Joanna Scott: Have you ever gone back to an old short story—found it to be actually three stories underdeveloped and torn apart the original in order to create at least one powerful one (at least in the eyes of the writer)?
Scott: I've gone back to old stories, and I've rewritten them as new stories. I've actually rewritten them as novels. *Arrogance* began as a story. I was determined after my second novel to go back to stories, so I began a story about the girl who had accused Egon Schiele of perversity, but then I found myself dealing with such immensely rich material, and so fascinated by the characters who were just hinted at in the story, that I stuck with it and wrote a novel. But I like the idea of ripping up one story to make three stories. That's productive.

Washington, DC: With so many books now written, is it any easier? Is there familiarity in the sources of inspiration? Is each book still a new challenge, or are there patterns you recognize in the writing that help you through it?

Scott: It's something I have been asking myself in recent years. Is this getting easier, or not? I think mostly not is the answer to that question. If anything it's getting harder.

I've been spending my days wandering through Florence, gazing at great art, and thinking about the muscular expressive art of a great artist like Michelangelo and the quieter restrained art of a great artist like del Sarto. He was called the artist *senza errore*, the artist who makes no mistakes. And I have found myself wanting to strive for that kind of gentle perfection, the restraint, the polish, a more tranquil beauty. Perhaps less expressive beauty, but still provocative and mysterious.

So, the general aesthetic challenges I set myself hopefully get harder. I want them to be harder. The blank space between the end of one book and the beginning of the next is just as blank as ever. But I think I've learned some things over the years.

Burns: One of the things I like about your work is how expansive it feels. It's not at all a close first-person voice. It feels like George Eliot to me. Do you think that kind of voice is less common these days? Why do you like it?
Scott: Probably what's generating that sense is that I move between characters. My first two books I was very close to my main character, stuck inside their head. And then with *Arrogance* I broke into many different voices. I introduce many different characters, and that helped me to develop the confidence to move between different characters, between different voices.

But once I wrote *Arrogance*, I was done with that form. I don't want to repeat myself. I'm just getting close to finishing up a new novel right now, and it feels like, That's it. I'm done. I'll never write another book. And the only way I can write another book is to tell myself, I'm going to do something different. Even as I'm learning from what I'm writing, I have to leave the work behind and start from scratch. I feel that very strongly with my work. I don't want to keep writing the same book. Or even if I did want to, I wouldn't have the discipline to do that. Some writers have done just that, and have done it successfully over thousands of pages. I want to keep trying out new things, new forms, learn something I didn't know before.

Washington, DC: Can you tell us who your favorite authors are, both current and past?
Scott: There's the short list and the long list. Some of the contemporary writers I feel nourished by include Nadine Gordimer, Maureen Howard, W. G. Sebald, John Berger, Ian McEwan, Don DeLillo, Steve Erikson, Ricki

Docornet, Michael Cunningham, Edward P. Jones, Kathryn Davis. All these writers share one thing, and that's the ability to do something new with narrative form.

In terms of writers I keep going back to, the list would include Dickens, Woolf, Chekhov, Faulkner, Beckett, Calvino. To name a few. I find my interest in them keeps changing, depending on what I'm working on or what my concerns are for a particular project, or for my life as a teacher. So one year I become absolutely obsessed with Chekhov. The next year it's Beckett. The next year it's Faulkner. But at any given time I'll be naming different writers who I feel are my strongest influences. The list keeps changing as I keep changing.

Washington, DC: You seem so very prolific! How do you do it?
Scott: I don't feel prolific. I've been writing for twenty years, and how many books do I have? Seven? Is that prolific?

Okay, if I am prolific, it's because writing is a nervous habit for me. I can't help it. I do it, and I do it obsessively. I'm cursed. It drives my family crazy.

Burns: Thanks so much, Joanna, for visiting *Off the Page*.

Catching Up with Joanna Scott: A Profile

Daniel Nester / 2007

From *Poets & Writers Magazine*, January/February 2007. Reprinted by permission of the publisher, Poets & Writers, Inc., 90 Broad Street, Suite 2100, New York, NY 10004. www.pw.org.

The clouds hang low in the sky on a gray afternoon in Rochester, New York, as fiction writer Joanna Scott sits at her desk in the half-finished attic of her 1920s house. Several prints adorn the walls around her: Edward Hopper's famous *Nighthawks* on one side; a few by Egon Schiele—the inspiration for *Arrogance* (Linden Press, 1990), Scott's fictional account of the Austrian artist's life—on the other.

There, in the attic, Scott looks through a window—"my future," she says, laughing, and then, glancing at the flat-screen monitor atop the desk where she writes, adds, "and the past is in front of me." Anyone who has kept track of Scott's writing career, which began twenty years ago with the publication of her debut novel, *Fading, My Parmacheene Belle* (Ticknor and Fields, 1987), knows that she need not worry about her future going out the proverbial window. In fact, her future looks rather bright compared to the gray Rochester sky. Just last month, *Everybody Loves Somebody*, her ninth book and second collection of short stories—having received the usual prepublication buzz in the form of *Kirkus* and *Publishers Weekly* starred reviews, as well as the kind of "writer's writer" word of mouth that is the stuff of authorial dreams—was published by Back Bay Books, a division of Little, Brown.

More than a decade in the making, *Everybody Loves Somebody* is Scott's first story collection since *Various Antidotes* (Henry Holt, 1994), which was a finalist for the PEN/Faulkner Award. Scott says she worked on the ten stories very slowly between the writing of the novels *The Manikin* (Henry Holt, 1996), which was a Pulitzer Prize finalist; *Make Believe* (Little, Brown, 2000);

Tourmaline (Little, Brown, 2002); and *Liberation* (Little, Brown, 2005). "I had to be very patient, bide my time, and let the stories grow," she says.

Indeed, the stories grew from the same mixture of historical, scientific, and sometimes oddball sources that inspired the language and settings of her novels, which range from a whaling ship transporting slaves in the mid-nineteenth century to a deteriorating mansion inhabited by an aging taxidermist in upstate New York in the 1920s to the Italian Island of Elba off the coast of Tuscany.

Everybody Loves Somebody is, simply, a collection of love stories. In fact, it is billed as "a history of love in the twentieth century," although the writing in the book is certainly not as systematic as the marketing text makes it sound. "I did have this general idea about the way I wanted to move through time and certain subjects I was going to address," she says, but at the same time she insists that her writing process has never involved strict outlines. "It might be a glance out the window, it might be a bit of conversation overheard, it might be a nugget from an old newspaper, which is actually how this book of short stories was generated," she says. "Looking for something else, some other kind of information in old newspapers, I just ended up being transfixed by the stories I read that became the kernel of some of the stories in the collection."

While Scott's less-than-systematic process can lead her and her fictional characters to some unexpected places, just as often it can stymie her writing altogether. "I do throw away a lot—there are a lot of false starts," she says. "Some of those false starts I actually return to years later, if I happen to save them—but I usually don't because I'm very disorganized. They might somehow become fodder for a story in some weird way."

Take, for instance, "Heaven and Hell," the first story in *Everybody Loves Somebody*, which depicts an overlong wedding kiss between a bride and her bridegroom just after the end of World War I. A couple of years ago, Scott says, she had been "transfixed by songs, ballads, folk songs—just songs that tell stories," including Bob Dylan's version of "Froggie Went A-Courtin,'" from his 1992 covers album, *Good as I Been to You*. The song, about the wedding of a frog and a mouse attended by various rodents, reptiles, and insects, does not have a happy ending: After nineteen verses, the frog is swallowed by a duck, and the mouse is eaten by a cat. "It just got to me," she says, laughing.

While she set out to write a novel about the song, she ultimately couldn't make anything of it and put it aside. But still, "in weird ways," as she puts it, those efforts became the basis for "Heaven and Hell," a thirteen-page story that takes place with the newlyweds locked in an amorous embrace. The point of view shifts several times—from the bride's righteous uncle (who raised her since she was a child) to her hapless father (who is locked in a windowless bathroom during the ceremony) to various guests at the wedding, including one child who has wandered off, nearly drowning in the sea, and another who tries to eat a cicada. Although Scott insists that she can't explain how the song influenced the story, perhaps a partial answer can be found in the bee that hovers around the kissing couple—an ominous plot point upon which the narrative pivots from character to character, each with his own unique perspective and distinctive voice.

"One of the things I love about reading fiction is the music of the voice created, especially an idiosyncratic voice," Scott says. "I work hard to create a distinctive voice, I suppose. If that voice is confident enough, then the confines of that voice make the music happen for me. That would be the metaphor for it, in the sense that the rules of the sentence I get from the character's voice. And if I have a sense of that, then it's almost as if I'm trying to keep up with that voice."

It's no surprise, then, that Scott doesn't write character sketches or plot out her stories beforehand. "I know other writers who do that and do it very productively," she says. "But it takes away the organic quality of the narrative for me. I have to follow from the first sentence and not from a previous perception that I am then enacting in some way. I want to be able to put in motion this character, and then one thing follows another. I think the sense that fiction can cast its spell has to do with an inevitable quality that we can feel in narrative—whether it's a fractured, fragmented narrative or a single-paragraph kind of narrative. I think we love the feeling that it's moving in an inexorable way, and yet full of surprises.

"Somebody was quoting to me the other day from Chekhov: 'What it takes is compassion, compassion, compassion,'" Scott says. "Perhaps it's the theatrical sense of fiction that I have—I like a cast of diverse characters on the page. I still love that—you know, to fall deeply into the mind, to experience thought. But I definitely like a limber narrator who can move between different points of view. With short stories, of course, I can end and then begin with another character. I guess it's partly an attempt to find out what it's like to be inside someone else's head."

Scott's attempt at imagining the interior lives of others began in Darien, Connecticut, where she was born in 1960 and grew up with three older brothers, secretly writing to fight the isolation she felt as the youngest sibling—and only daughter. "I was not included in much that went on among them, and this forced me to try to make my isolation exciting," she said in a profile published in the January/February 1996 issue of this magazine. As an undergraduate at Trinity College in the early 1980s, Scott studied English literature with fiction writers Stephen Minot and Thalia Selz, both of whom encouraged her to write. During this time she spent a semester in Rome studying Renaissance literature and Italian film and then enrolled for a year at Barnard College. After graduating in 1983, Scott moved to New York City, where she worked as an assistant to Geri Thoma at the Elaine Markson Literary Agency and received an informal education in the inner workings of the publishing industry. Soon thereafter she left New York for Brown University's graduate writing program, where she worked with such luminaries as Robert Coover, Susan Sontag, and John Hawkes, with whom she had a mentorship. But her connection to Thoma was not lost—she would eventually serve as Scott's agent.

After receiving her MA in 1985, Scott, unsure of which direction her writing should take, stayed on at Brown to teach creative writing to undergraduates. She also started writing a novel that began as a story during her final semester. Tired of the criticism that was such an integral part of the graduate workshops, "tired of having to go back" to rework her stories, Scott began writing the novel in a less controlled, more inspired way. "I just wrote it, and I didn't even come up for air," she says. "I didn't even know I was writing a novel." What began as a story with a unique first sentence became the first chapter of *Fading, My Parmacheene Belle*, "and it sort of launched my whole career," she says.

That sentence is worth a closer look, since in many ways it's a perfect example of Scott's realistic, precise, elegant storytelling, and it also bears many of the elements of her later work, including compelling, albeit off-kilter, characters.

"I will tell you exactly how it was one day I said to my companion Gibble, 'I am alone here, I need a wife,' and he sent on the order without an adequate forewarning, he just breathed with a panting effort, those pockets beneath his jowls throbbing like the gills of a river bass laid out in a pail."

Scott's debut novel was almost universally praised for its portrayal of an old man who struggles to come to terms with the death of his wife after fifty-three years of marriage and hooks up with a fifteen-year-old prostitute. The *Chicago Tribune* called it a "virtuoso performance"; the *New York Times Book Review* claimed it was "bucolic and biblical" and that "Scott's unusual imagination promises a rich future in writing."

In the years that followed, Scott proved the *Times* correct by receiving a Guggenheim Fellowship, which came on the heels of her second novel, *The Closest Possible Union* (Ticknor and Fields, 1988); the Lillian Fairchild Award for contribution to the arts in 1990; the Richard and Hinda Rosenthal Foundation Award from the Academy of Arts and Letters in 1991; a MacArthur "Genius" Fellowship in 1992; and a Lannan Literary Award in 1999. For the past twenty years she has taught writing and literature at the University of Rochester.

And yet one could still call Scott one of the best-kept secrets in American literature. Her books sell pretty well and attract a good-sized readership, and they all remain in print, but so far the real mainstream success, the "breakthrough" book, has eluded her. "Of course we'd love Joanna to find the readership she deserves," says Reagan Arthur, Scott's editor at Little, Brown for the past five years. "It's hard to know when or how that lightning will strike."

A "major prize or significant critical outpouring" might do the trick, Arthur says, and cites Penelope Fitzgerald's being "discovered" after the *New York Times Book Review* front-page review of *The Blue Flower* (Houghton Mifflin, 1997) as an example. But Scott keeps a healthy perspective on the prospect of literary stardom. "I've had independent film options, very interesting prospects, some things that might still be rolling along," she says. "I would love to be the kernel of inspiration for someone else."

A Conversation with Maureen Howard

Joanna Scott / 2010

From *The Believer*, no. 71 (May 1, 2010). Reprinted by permission.

Joanna Scott is the author of two collections of stories and eight novels, most recently *Follow Me* (Little, Brown, 2009). She has lived with her family in Italy, pursuing her fiction, but is settled in upstate New York, where she teaches at the University of Rochester. Joanna is a recipient of a MacArthur Fellowship, a Lannan Award, a Guggenheim Fellowship, and the Rosenthal Prize from the American Academy of Arts and Letters.

Maureen Howard is the author of nine novels and a memoir, *Facts of Life*, which won the National Book Critics Circle Award. *The Rags of Time* (Viking, 2009) is the last in a series of novels celebrating the four seasons. She is the recipient of the Academy Award in Literature from the Academy of Arts and Letters. She was born in Bridgeport, Connecticut, and made her way to New York where she has lived for many years with the comfort of family. She teaches at Columbia University's School of the Arts.

Scott and Howard met when they were seated next to each other at dinner at a Houston writing festival one night in 1991, and continued talking at a PEN/Faulkner gathering in Washington, DC, later that year. Joanna was expecting her first child. Maureen and Joanna have been talking children and writing ever since. Their girls are now well grown. The exchange that follows took place over email in the winter of 2009–2010.

Joanna Scott: Maureen, I've been thinking about your memoir *Facts of Life* and its relationship to the fictional remembering that goes on in your new *Rags of Time*. I wonder if I'm right to sense that the two books share an energizing tension? On the one hand, a home is a writer's necessary refuge—the work gets done behind a closed door. On the other hand, a home can be a "stifling refuge" (a phrase you use in *Facts of Life*), and the world outside the door, with its layered history, is always beckoning. The first thing your fictional writer does in *The Rags of Time* is to head out, away from home, into Central Park.

Maureen Howard: The exploration of place: I say that as though to introduce a classroom spin. Today we will concern ourselves with Flannery O'Connor's confinement to Milledgeville, Georgia, where she discovered the saved and the damned; to Naipaul's childhood in Trinidad which became sacred to him in England. Well, if I seem unable to swing free of Bridgeport, even now recalling the chug-chug of factories in WWII, it may be to reconsider the best of times. In *Natural History*, both a novel and history of my city, I romanticized the myths of Barnum's Winter Quarters, and the secrets of City Hall. These many years in New York I'm quite at home, know the bus routes and where to scout out the Extra Virgin! olive oil, but often turn to the memory bank in a mix of melancholy, mockery, and affection hoping I have not overinvested in the double feature at the Rialto, the parish church.

I envy your possession of the island of Elba in *Liberation*. In *Follow Me* you place a map of the Tuskee River to guide both the writer and the reader of the novel. It becomes your Yoknapatawpha County. Mind if I call in the gentleman writer? I must believe that when we leave home, we are ready to leap over the gender gap.

JS: Yes, it's a wonderful freedom we have on the page. We can start by presuming that anything's possible, and then we step across those borders that in the real world might be impassable. But wherever we go, we take the baggage of our memories with us. Your fictional New York is really a version of Bridgeport, stretched to fill a bigger map. That makes perfect sense. New places mirror our first formative experiences when we were figuring out how to get from one address to another. "Pay attention to here and now" your fictional writer reminds herself as she heads out once again into Central Park: "Delighted to be released from Bridgeport, just for the day." But still "that old stuff" presses in. Bridgeport won't let you forget it.

MH: Actually, she pastes that line on a photo of her parents walking arm in arm on Fifth Avenue, pleased with their adventure just for the day. That old stuff, but then again, Make it New, the old adage of modernism is with me still. A vintage bottle hasn't lost its fine nose. To discover a form for each story—where to put the journalistic scrap, how to emboss the surface of setting, be it my Park of the new millennium or Frederick Law Olmsted's plan for the

Greensward, or the retreat of the Germans in your *Liberation*. We ask the reader to follow the turns of narrative, but if you put a coin in the slot, there are multiple views which may contain the personal story. Collage: the early paste-ups, the background of brush strokes, history fractured with today's news. I think of Sebald walking the byways of East Anglia, milling history for the daily bread of his writing. His discovery of place is more than setting, more than local history; his discovery of past and adjacent lives is self-discovery. In an early collection of stories, you wrote of historical figures—Dorothea Dix, Charlotte Corday—appropriated their lives to suit your purpose.

JS: Really, I think they appropriated me to suit their purposes! That's usually the case with my fiction. There I am, just walking along, wrapped up in my own petty troubles, and I hear ghosts whispering from the shadows. I like the feeling of that kind of discovery, when we're caught by surprise, when the world reveals a portion of itself unexpectedly. But it's not enough for fiction writers to collect stories and retell them, is it? Your notion of collage (something you enact visually in your books, with images and blocks of text) is beautifully apt—the past fractured with the present. Writing fiction begins with a process of fracturing. We chip away at known reality, take pieces of it, and then set off to elaborate and assemble in order to try to press toward the part of experience that resists knowing yet tempts us with the possibility of understanding. And because a thing that is individually and lovingly made reveals aspects of the person who made it, the end product of this process of assembling, the collage that is fiction, involves self-portraiture. I'm taking the long route back to your idea about the writer's personal involvement. The author may be absent from the work, but she's left her dirty fingerprints all over the pages. I see you, Maureen, in your *Rags*, not just in your fictional writer but in the very structure and style of the book. You've made something that can contain different points of view, contrasting impressions, and your characteristic blend of past and present. And I sense that behind this multiplicity is an author who remains acutely concerned about the future.
MH: Which future? An agreeable future of nuclear deterrence plotted in Geneva? The future of the great melt? A revival of the gold standard? Of my grandchildren who, I like to believe, live in a state of innocence? Or the future of our stories, the weight of their fancy? Ranting again, powerless, well aware my soapbox is cheap wood that splinters. I stole that line from Sinclair Lewis, gave it to the writer in *Rags*. Thinking about the responsibility of fiction recently, I came across a prescription for searching out the word: "The word that could stand as all the words covering the page, a word

which if not truth itself, may perchance hold truth enough to help the moral discovery which should be the object of every tale."—Joseph Conrad. If that sounds heavy duty, so be it. Post it over my desk with a photo of Ethel Merman belting out "Let Me Entertain You." Concerned about the future? Or did you mean the future of the book?

JS: I like to imagine Joseph Conrad and Ethel Merman sharing your wall. About the future, it's an elusive prey for those of us who work with narrative. Isn't it related to the notion of "moral discovery"? I'm reminded of a beautifully intimate production of Chekhov's *Three Sisters* I recently saw up at the Stratford Festival in Ontario. As I walked away from the theater, I found myself worrying about the disappointments ahead for those characters, as though the play hadn't really finished. And this made me think about the consequences of all choices that we dare to make. I felt that I was more alert to the impact of my present actions, thanks to Chekhov. If nothing else, we come out of our immersion in an artfully told story with a new sense of urgency. Time is short, and there's so much to do. Time is short, and you've managed to complete the whole of your Four Seasons. It was a daring thing to take on, Maureen. Did you know what you were getting into when you started writing *A Lover's Almanac*?

MH: I knew the stories would continue, the time allotted in the earliest season might not be enough. We were heading to the millennium, a date of reckoning so the media thought, the computer folk, too. I had no crystal ball, just faith that our stories must go on as they always have—in the cave, the schoolroom, on screen, and in a generosity of time offered by the novel. I had come across Benjamin Franklin's *Poor Richard's Almanac* portioning out the year with entertainments, fanciful stories yet always wise in Franklin's advice. I have an astronomer friend who calculates the heavens for *The Farmer's Almanac*, so the phases of the moon, sighting of the North Star are exact. My *Almanac* is a Winter story of late love and young love in need of a thaw. Continuing themes? I presumed I could take Audubon's ambition in *Big As Life*, place his magnificent folio of American Birds next to my birdwatcher's sketches: his big drama, her accuracy of singular observation. Perhaps I thought four seasons would see me out. Out of the workroom into Central Park is all I mean.

JS: Did you begin with themes then? How did the characters emerge? Looking back at the beginning of *Lover's Almanac*, I wonder which came first, the name "Louise Moffet," or her predicament?

MH: Little Miss Muffet sat on a tuffet. Not frightened, my Louise Moffett. She packed up, left the farm with her portfolio of drawings, flagged down the bus to New York. I have long been interested in that promise, the bold investment in the future. Way back in *Bridgeport Bus* I mapped the route to the big city. The predicament? Will she make it? Of more importance, will she make a life? We can call upon characters we once called heroines—Wharton's Lily Bart, Esther in *Bleak House*, Doris Lessing's *Martha Quest*, your Sally Werner in *Follow Me*—all get on the bus for the chapters that lie ahead. Reading Sally's story, I feel you are writing in ballad form, each part of her journey gathering new lyrics, new entries in her story. Sorting playful from upward and onward, taking the trip each time is the serious game of fiction.

JS: Yes, the journey continues from writer to writer. *The Ballad of Sally Werner* was in fact one of my early working titles. I never meant it to be a final title, but I did have the model of the ballad in mind as I was writing. And a bus really is the perfect narrative vehicle for fiction. Did I ever tell you about the bus trip I took across country when I was eighteen? I went from Portland, Oregon, to New York City with seven dollars in my pocket, a jar of peanut butter, and a loaf of bread. I still have vivid memories of the people I met along the way. That would have been a novel, if I'd known how to write one back then. I had to read Beckett first, and you, and plant myself in the basement of a library for a few years. Also, I had to sharpen my skills on my typewriter, a big pink IBM electric I bought used on Twenty-Seventh Street in New York. And then I had to catch up and learn the functions of various word processing programs. So how does technology come into play? This is a subject that you recently brought up in an email.

MH: Cleaning up my back room after years of work in progress, I came across an article from the *New York Times*, August 19, 2002, testimony to my curiosity in new adventures for readers: a photo of words swirling on a wall with sound effects; an inset photo of traffic on a highway, presumably New York City. Interesting bricolage, but what rocked me was the commentary of a professor at UCLA on electronic writing: "For centuries literature has been delivered in a vehicle with a narrow sensory interface: the print book." She welcomed "a richer sensory input." Joanna, do you feel impoverished, undernourished by the page? Do you ever stifle a sob at the end of a moving passage? Not the passing of Little Nell; perhaps Lily Bart embracing death; or laugh at the endless physical impairments of Beckett's fortunate family Lynch in *Watt*? Want to throw a feeble story across the room? Anyway: same article pictures Robert Coover in a virtual-reality chamber at Brown, computer-generated lines of *Moby-Dick* swirling on the walls. "I'm not convinced that it's going to work to deliver literary art," Coover says, "but I don't want to be excluded from it." Nor do I, and I'm particularly taken by that shot of traffic overprinted with Melville's words—"There now is your insular city of the Manhattoes, belted round by wharves . . ." "It's extreme downtown is the Battery . . ." and so forth as the writer jumps ship for the many stops along the way of his great adventure. Recently I sense you have been out of sorts with the well-told, so, does the cure await in the interactive?

JS: I think what you're referring to is my occasional impolite expression of impatience with tales that threaten to oversimplify experience. It's not that I object to the "well-told," as you put it. I love those tales that flaunt their elegance (the stories of Isak Dinesen and Angela Carter come to mind). But I also love wild explorations of madness. I feel a little less alone when I encounter characters who are working through befuddlement. We'll never run out of things to say about the struggle to make sense of confusion. It could be that the notion of the interactive is making narrative more flexible in its rendering of groping thought. But I don't think we've come close to realizing all the possibilities of the printed page.

MH: Poor old printed page sporting its careful, or do I mean conservative fiction, at times chancing an energetic style, lacking the risk of imagination. Pat, pat, turn the page for there the reader will find the assurance of ongoing narrative without seeming misdirection, no sidebars. Except, of course, there's Powers and Wallace (RIP), Jeanette Winterson, Zadie Smith, Belano just now—his doorstop as postmortem; three voices on the triangulated page of Coetzee's *Diary of a Bad Year.*

JS: Are you saying here that a story that charges toward its end is necessarily conservative? You're arguing in favor of a narrative made up of digressions? But I wonder if those sidebars can be deceptive. I think of the footnotes in Nabokov's *Pale Fire*—these end up moving the plot forward in sneaky ways. Each of Nabokov's apparent digressions manages to add to the suspense. But maybe that's your point. Suspense can come in many flavors. It isn't just generated by a sequence of actions. There might be suspense in the delays of a meandering narrative, or in the invention of competing voices. As a reader, I love to get caught up in paragraphs that are full of vivacious details. Confusion can be very suspenseful, if we're able to move through the murk. I'm convinced that the most essential suspense in fiction is generated within each sentence. There might even be a suspenseful element to this conversation!

MH: As in table tennis? But you are far more agile of mind. You do actually ride horses, set the post high. Where might we end? Not in discord, not likely. Your probing is inspired yet reasonable. Your consideration of what's genuine in a story right on; while I mouth off on the ingenuous: The weight of discourse in George Eliot; and, after her first novel, the serious play of Virginia Woolf, particularly the endgame of *Between the Acts*. Having parodied all of England's history from prehistoric man, half human, half ape to a day in June 1939 when the blitz had destroyed a good deal of London, she brings the panoramic down to a domestic scene between a disaffected husband and wife: "Then the curtain rose. They spoke." The simplicity of small sentences, their weight. The reader does not have to know that Mrs. Woolf was about to write a last note to her husband—"I want to tell you that you have given me complete happiness . . . ," that she put stones in her pockets to end her own story. Revealing diaries, letters, *A Sketch of the Past*, the brave adventure of her writing life were over though she never appeared unmasked in her fiction, a postmodern gesture.

The search for form is dangerous as a cut into stone that makes or defaces the sculptor's work; or like the tailor's stitches ripped to let out the binding collar of linear time. As for your postpartum sorrow for Chekhov's abandoned provincials, their future may be imagined by the writer. Perhaps a Scott appropriation on the fate of Uncle Vanya's medical career?

JS: There's an idea—Uncle Vanya moves to upstate New York. Your last question reminds me to consider dimension as well as direction in narrative. Maybe it's in the depths of their characters, in the hidden sources of singular voices, where writers like Eliot and Woolf and Chekhov establish the assurance of continuity. And at the same time they let us experience the potential for arbitrary turns. But I wonder about your comment that the "search for form" is dangerous. Are you talking about the danger of losing the reader if we shake up the form, or the danger of losing our minds?

MH: Oh, we're performing for the reader: at times a high wire act; at times the comfort of telling a fireside tale, the love story again. As for losing my mind? It was lost long ago. I gave over so thoroughly to the pursuit of fiction. You write reviews and criticism, though I think your devotion is to stories, to the construction of novels in particular. Is it addictive? I have seldom taken a break that wasn't claimed by the pleasures or problems of family life. Or teaching: I recall being envious of you the semester when you read just Dickens with your class. I've never had the opportunity to do that: delve.

JS: I'm surprised that you would say you don't delve. What about Woolf, or Cather? Or P. T. Barnum, for that matter? Or Olmsted or Audubon? I'd call you a supreme delver! And I know you're thinking about the possibility of delving into something new. We talked about this the other day on the phone. You've just finished years of an ongoing project. What's next? the world asks. And you're asking, what do we do when we're not writing? Well, there's always life to keep us busy. And we can read about other people's lives. If we're lucky, we might be able to stand close to paintings and examine the brushwork. Some of us go to parties or travel or play music or drink. I admit I find it hard to know what to do with myself, or at least with my imagination, when I'm between projects. But yes, it's a time to get recharged, to gather up influences and discover what we missed while we were absorbed in our dreams.

MH: What are you working on? I call that a provocative question. As though the dough must be rising, if bread not already in the oven. I'm about to teach a course in self-portraits, written portraits of course, but also a look-see at the many self-portraits of Rembrandt—costumed, flamboyant when young, signs of illness in old age. And that moving study by Agnes Martin, revealing herself naked in old age. I was ticked off by a review of my *Rags* that reported me as eighty. I am seventy-nine, says so in the virtual page of my story. I might try my hand at biography, not the bio pics I've loved writing, but fear I might lose the years left to another life. Thomas Hardy went back to poetry, but I'll not try friends with attachments of my versification. Questions: Add to a book of stories never collected over the years? That's the easy way out. I do have a model, a book like Fitzgerald's *The Crack Up*, the confession, arrogance intact, pathos of letters to his daughter. Delete Bridgeport? I'm losing my mind, as you suggest.

JS: Those are all wonderful possibilities. And I'm so heartened by your determination. I read just the other morning that the last bookstore in Laredo, Texas, has closed. Now if you live in Laredo and want to browse in a bookstore, you need to drive 150 miles to San Antonio. And the cover story of this week's *New York Times* magazine: a bestselling writer farms out his ideas to coauthors while devoting most of his own time to marketing the franchise of his fiction. We'll see how it plays out. But you're right, the point is to press on with new explorations. Until we give up on words altogether, we'll need literature to keep teaching us how meaning can be made.

MH: Or sought in the next lap of our stories. *Yes, a voice comes to me in the dark. Scripto ergo sum.*

JS: Well, I'm impressed, Maureen. You're looking forward toward a new book though your seventy-nine-year-old self hasn't even completed the year. I'll be turning fifty this summer; you'll be turning eighty. So what if we can't keep track of our errant minds? We must celebrate! I was supposed to hang upside down from a trapeze on my forty-fifth birthday. Just my luck, a storm moved in while I was waiting to climb the ladder, a bolt of lightning lit up the sky, and my trapeze swing was cancelled. Maybe we should try that high-wire act you mentioned earlier? Wouldn't it be something to be as fearless as Philippe Petit, who walked on a tightrope from the top of one twin tower to the other? I hear he does occasional reprises on a low rope in Washington Square. He also can push a baby in a stroller while riding a unicycle. Maybe we could learn how to do that.

MH: I sign off now. Only words in my teetering balance. *In the middle of the journey of our life . . . Stately plump Buck Mulligan . . . I was born . . . Lolita, light of my life, fire of my loins . . . I will arise and go now, and go to Innisfree . . . In my younger and more vulnerable days . . . And God called the light day and the darkness light . . . I was born . . . Mrs. Dalloway said she would buy the flowers herself.*

Joanna Scott—Author Interview

M. E. Wood / 2010

Published in BellaOnline: The Voice of Women. M. E. Wood lives in Eastern Ontario, Canada. Reprinted by permission.

Writing takes time and perseverance. It always amazes me when I learn a writer's background stories. How they manage to mesh their personal and professional lives and still have time to explore other interests. Following suit, Joanna is married, has two lovely daughters, works as an English professor in upstate New York and has managed to have nine publishable books served up to the public. And some horseback jumping thrown in for fun. Enjoy!

Moe E. Wood: Looking back, did you choose the writing profession, or did the profession choose you? When did you "know" you were a writer?
Joanna Scott: I was addicted to imaginative play as a child and wasn't ready to stop playing when I grew older. For a while, I kept at it in secret; then I discovered that I could keep losing myself in those unreal worlds of my imagination by writing fiction.

Moe: What inspires you?
Joanna Scott: Conversation, in all forms (with people, with books and newspapers, with the past).

Moe: Every writer has a method to their writing. On a typical writing day, how would you spend your time?
Joanna Scott: I've lost my old routines. These days I snatch time at my desk between other commitments, whenever I can. But I'm learning that imagination can be nourished by varied commitments.

Moe: How long does it take for you to complete a book you would allow someone to read? Do you write right through or do you revise as you go along?

Joanna Scott: The computer has made it too easy to block and delete and replace one word with another! I rarely finish a sentence (like this one) without backtracking and revising in an attempt to achieve greater clarity. Increasingly, I write in a circular fashion and return to the beginning of something whenever I set out to move forward. Somehow I manage to accumulate pages. I've finished some books within a year's time; others have taken several years.

Moe: When you sit down to write is any thought given to the genre or type of readers?

Joanna Scott: I try to attend to the requirements of the specific work, to follow its unique rules and make something solid and integral. But I'm always hoping to give readers something that's nourishing, absorbing, and startling.

Moe: When it comes to plotting, do you write freely or plan everything in advance?

Joanna Scott: My intentions spin off in the craziest directions! I can barely keep up with them. I might make plans, but they're all shredded by page 2.

Moe: What kind of research do you do before and during a new book? Do you visit the places you write about?

Joanna Scott: My methods for accumulating information keep getting stranger: for recent books, I've started with my private dream of a real place. I've had to see it in my mind first and describe it with my own words before I read about it. I read about it after I've already described it at length. Then I go back to the pages I've written. Armed with some facts, I gently correct my mistakes and keep writing. And then, when it's possible, I go to explore the place—I wander its streets and climb its mountains and skin my knees trying to climb up walls and peer into backyards. Sometimes I get into trouble for this.

Moe: Do you ever suffer from writer's block? If yes, what measures do you take to get past it?

Joanna Scott: Even when my confidence flags, I'll keep spitting out words— nonsense, junk, graffiti—for better or worse.

Moe: What do you hope readers gain, feel, or experience when they read one of your books for the first time?

Joanna Scott: Certain works of fiction have made me feel less afraid of the intense complexities of experience, and so I try to write books that might do the same for others.

Moe: Can you share three things you've learned about the business of writing since your first publication?
Joanna Scott: Well, there's more sting involved than I'd expected. But when it comes to the business, I remain willfully naive.

Moe: What is your latest release about?
Joanna Scott: I'd been reading through old newspapers and wondering about the anonymous lives on the outskirts of history. And I'm always wondering about strangers I see at a glance. I went in search of them—these ghosts of the past and the strangers of the present. I found some of them in the imagined worlds of the short stories in *Everybody Loves Somebody*. I've tried to convey the intensity of their experiences—their passions and successes and defeats.

Moe: What kind of books do you like to read?
Joanna Scott: Books that make me more aware. For example, some recent exciting immersions include Saramago's *Blindness*, John Berger's *King*, Maureen Howard's *The Silver Screen*, W. G. Sebald's *Austerlitz*.

Moe: When you're not writing what do you do for fun?
Joanna Scott: Sailing over jumps on horseback, holding on for dear life.

Moe: New writers are always trying to glean advice from those with more experience. What suggestions do you have for new writers?
Joanna Scott: To quote my first editor, who was quoting a friend of his, who was quoting Samuel Beckett: "Tell them to be very, very careful." I take this as a warning to think twice before casting an idea as the truth.

Moe: If you weren't a writer what would you be?
Joanna Scott: Unsteady.

The Masking Art
of the Biographical Novel

Michael Lackey / 2014

From *Truthful Fictions: Conversations with American Biographical Novelists*, ed. Michael Lackey (New York and London: Bloomsbury, 2014), 217–29.

Michael Lackey: Let me start by telling you about the nature of this project. I'm trying to figure out why, starting in the 1980s, so many prominent writers began to author biographical novels. I am also trying to define the nature of this genre of fiction. Can you start by explaining what led you to write a novel about the Austrian artist Egon Schiele? And can you explain why you decided to write a novel rather than a biography or a scholarly study?

Joanna Scott: I was still in my twenties, and I was feeling very energetic as a writer. *Arrogance* is my third book. With my first novel, I discovered the fun of writing away from myself, in the voice of a narrator utterly different from me. With my second novel, *The Closest Possible Union*, narrated by a captain's apprentice on an illegal slave ship, I began my lifelong quest to mine history for lost stories. Coming out of that book, I was wondering what I might write next. It was during that time, a twilight period between books, that I went to an exhibit at the Museum of Modern Art in New York. The show focused on *fin de siècle* Vienna, the art, music, and architecture of the time, which was a very rich period. Most of the work on display was by the artist Gustav Klimt. But there was a back room with drawings by a lesser-known artist named Egon Schiele. While I was in the room, people were walking through expressing some startled reactions to Schiele's work. One couple stopped in front of *Self Portrait of the Artist Masturbating*, and the man looked at the woman and said, "Would you buy a used car from that guy?" "Ho ho ho!" they laughed. But when I looked at this portrait and then looked back at the people, I was struck by their condescension. I was also struck by Schiele's ferocity of expression. It just made me wonder about him.

I didn't know anything about Schiele, so I went home and started to explore. I paid a visit to the art library at my university to see what I could find out. At that point, Schiele really was not well known in this country. And there weren't many books about him available in English. I did find a book by Alessandra Comini about his time in prison, along with a translation of his diary from this period. I read these with intense interest, trying to understand the artist who had provoked the viewers in the back room of the Museum of Modern Art to be contemptuous.

In his diary, Schiele mentioned a girl he thought was his accuser. This caught my attention. I'm always on the lookout for lost stories that deserve attention, stories that have been forgotten or haven't been told. Also, following my experience with my previous novel, I was feeling the drive to investigate pivotal moments in history and see if there was more to say and tell. I will never stop wondering about the voices that have been suppressed or ignored. I found a suppressed voice in the girl Schiele thought was his accuser. Her story hadn't been told, as far as I knew, so I decided to tell a story about Schiele's time in prison from *her* perspective. To my surprise, the story kept going. The girl became the opening narrator of each chapter and gave me access into Schiele's life. She is as central to the book as he is.

Lackey: What ultimately made you settle on Schiele? In other words, what was it about him that made you think he is so pivotal?

Scott: I felt that the exposure Schiele was offering in his drawings was very daring. And the more I read about him, the more I admired the risks he was taking with his art. I wasn't totally won over by the work, but I was fascinated and impressed. It's important to remember that he died at the age of twenty-eight. He did incredible work as a young artist, in a relatively short amount of time. I would have *loved* to see the work he would have done as a more mature artist. His ambition didn't have much chance to evolve. So while I admire him, I also see some limitations in his work. But from the start, I admired his daring, and I felt that he was important to our time. Artists need to be able to take risks, we need to be able to make ourselves vulnerable, and I found a model in Schiele.

Lackey: One of the striking things about your novel is the relationship between Klimt and Schiele. Schiele initially admires Klimt, and he is certainly in Klimt's debt. But as the novel progresses, he becomes increasingly more critical of him. He thinks of Klimt as a bourgeois optimist, while Schiele adopts a much bleaker view of the world. Could you discuss that relationship in the novel?

Scott: Yes, and in a way you are probing a dirty little secret in the novel. I couldn't help but consider my own position as a young artist while I was writing the book. I wrote the book when I was twenty-eight—Schiele's age when he died. I felt his relationship to Klimt's more decorative, playful art was not without resonance in my own life. Schiele was passionate, dedicated, and very serious. As a young writer, I found the work of certain more established writers provocative and even nurturing, but I felt some impatience with the jokiness of the new postmodernism, the satire for satire's sake. Some of the playfulness seemed frivolous to me. In fact, as time goes on, I have more of a taste for lightness and playfulness in art. Back then, though, I wanted to write something more expressive than decorative. I was very serious, in my own way.

Lackey: Shifting to a different topic, there was a famous debate in 1968 with Robert Penn Warren, Ralph Ellison, and William Styron about the ethics and the wisdom of naming a protagonist in a novel after the original figure. Ellison praised Warren for changing Huey Long's name to Willie Stark in *All the King's Men* and he criticized Styron for naming Nat Turner after the original person in *The Confessions of Nat Turner.* Ellison's critique was twofold: naming the protagonist after the original would necessarily lead the author to misrepresent the complexity and details of the original figure, and it would make the novelist vulnerable to attack from historians. How would you respond to Ellison? Also, can you explain why you didn't write a novel loosely based on Schiele but change his name in order to give yourself more creative license? Were you tempted to do that at all?

Scott: No, weirdly it never occurred to me not to use his name. And that's something we could probe a little bit, though I'm not sure I can offer a good explanation. I could talk, and will, about certain precedents I think I had in mind as I was writing. But in terms of Ellison's critique here, that's a slippery road. It seems to me that if the name of a person is off limits, then why wouldn't the name of a place be off limits? Why wouldn't every verifiable fact be off limits?

Lackey: In *Invisible Man* he does exactly that. Many readers, for example, think that the Brotherhood in the novel is the Communist Party, but Ellison is absolutely insistent that it is not. As a symbol, the Brotherhood could be used to illuminate the Communist Party, but it could also illuminate many other organizations.

Scott: Absolutely, and it's significant that his main character does not have a name. Ellison makes sure we understand that a name can become fraught with meaning. It can carry dangerous cultural baggage. I respect his nervousness about naming. But then I'm all for keeping open as many doors as possible. If we say we can't use the name of a historical figure, why should I be able to use the name of a woman no one remembers but is inscribed on a nineteenth-century tombstone? And if I can't use her name, I can't use the name of the cemetery, and if I can't use the name of the cemetery, then I shouldn't be able to set down my characters at the Alamo, or in Times Square for that matter. All these names signify something unalterable. By appropriating them for fiction, I signal that I will alter them. I will do something other than what the historian does with them. I will reshape facts to create an imaginative experience rather than use them as supportive evidence. If we follow Ellison's restriction to its ultimate end, it's not just names that are sacrosanct. Words tend to come with their own baggage. So I can't use words! Then we are done. We end in silence. I suppose it is unfair to exaggerate the implications of the restriction to such an extent. But it's important to remember that every fiction writer is involved in an effort of distortion. As soon as we call something "a fiction," we are indicating that it cannot be relied upon for historical accuracy. Readers usually know to look elsewhere for historical accuracy, and if they don't, good luck to them. The deeper I got into writing *Arrogance*, the more my attention went to creating something new rather than repeating what was already known.

I find myself thinking about the artificial nature of fiction more than ever these days, and I keep coming back to the metaphor of the mask. I'm probably closer in spirit to a masked performer wandering through the fog of Venice during Carnivale than to a historian. Say someone is wearing a mask that recreates the face of Napoleon with leather and paint—you are not going to worry if the person wearing the mask is imitating Napoleon exactly, word for word, gesture for gesture. What is more interesting is the way that the mask is put into action and the dynamic relationship between the mask wearer and the mask itself. Sometimes fiction writers happen to wear a mask that resembles an identifiable historical figure, but it is the ingenuity of the performance rather than the precision of the resemblance that counts.

Lackey: Virginia Woolf had some very serious problems with the concept of the biographical novel, and I don't think she could have seen her way to it. She claims that it is illegitimate to mix fact and fiction. The novelist creates, whereas the biographer gives us fact, and if the writer were bound by fact, this would necessarily prohibit the artist from doing what he or she does, which is to create. So she wanted to make sure that she was going to protect the artist's freedom to create a living and breathing character. Do you agree with that?

Scott: I'll guess that Woolf's motive was to protect the freedom of the novelist rather than to define limits. And certainly in her own fiction she gives us many opportunities to consider how facts mix with the imaginative entities we have come to call "characters." I think of Mrs. Dalloway walking through London—through Woolf's fictional version of factual London. I also think of the panoply of voices in *The Waves*. The characters in that novel are given names and identities, but Woolf makes sure that we keep thinking about how identity is constructed with words. And if we pay attention to how names are given meaning, then we can start thinking about how unstable meaning is, how it is revised and even invented with every new sentence. It seems to me that Woolf was expressing concern with the way the past can be sneakily misrepresented in conventional historical fiction. Given her own experiment in *Orlando*, I would assume she wasn't worried about the brazen distortions of history in imaginative literature. And maybe she was also pointing to an inherent limitation of biography. We want to be able to trust that the facts in a biography will hold up to scrutiny. If the author of a biography, or of any historical work, has mixed fiction with the facts so the different genres are indistinguishable, then that can be problematic.

Of course, I can hear my historian friends reminding me that the act of interpretation is in itself creative and skews everything. It impacts our ability to ascertain causes, trajectories, patterns. But if we are thinking about the biographer's responsibility to the reader, and to the material, I have to agree with Woolf. Fiction does not mix well in a biographical soup. In the soup of the novel, however, fact is a basic ingredient. And I think, looking at Woolf's own fiction, she works beautifully with history. She may veil specific times and places and blur what we think we know about London in the 1920s, or an historical event like World War I, yet she manages to make these subjects newly vivid.

Lackey: And she veils them so she can give herself more creative freedom, so that she is not bound by these actual figures.

Scott: Yes, I don't want to be bound, but I am willing to use a much more transparent veil. I don't think we need to hide the relationship to the real or the factual. Fiction is always made up of stuff drawn from the past—even if the past is only yesterday. And I side with Defoe who says of *Robinson Crusoe* that his version is truer than history! Absolutely.

Lackey: Jay Parini makes a similar observation. In a conversation with Peter Ackroyd, Jay asked: "What's the difference between your biographies and your biographical novels?" Ackroyd said: "In my biographical novels I have to tell the truth."

Scott: Novelists have always been a little nervous about this, and we say it perhaps more fervently than we need to, that our made-up stories are truer than the truth.

Lackey: It gets a different kind of truth, doesn't it?

Scott: That's the goal. And in this Information Age, when the race is on to make ourselves immortal by gathering up all that can be known and making the facts work to our advantage, I feel a need to reassert that the inquiry of fiction has its own legitimacy. I just heard a talk last night in which a novelist came around to this very topic. His ambition, he said, is to get it right, to do a whole lot of research and make the fiction an accurate historical representation. My ambition is to get it wrong. Am I going to get in trouble for saying that? I want to make something new and intricately expressive, even as I try to honor the richness of the past. There's immense satisfaction in looking back into history and trying to find what is hidden. But the fundamental joy for me is in the act of invention.

Lackey: Russell Banks has an argument that might resonate with yours. He noted a consistency in biographies about John Brown. For most white writers, Brown is either insane or criminal. But for most black writers, he is a hero, almost a saint. Russell said that he began to realize that the biographers deal with the same facts, but they come up with radically different interpretations of the man. So he realized that there's something very naïve about assuming that facts give us an authoritative or accurate picture of history. As a novelist, he wanted to give us something very different, a kind of internal truth that cannot be converted into a metaphysical or absolute claim. To the contrary, he wanted to give us something much messier, something not nearly as codifiable. You can't fit human experience into easily categorizable systems, which is why he thinks there is something fundamentally false about the histories and biographies that presume we can do such a thing.

Scott: Since fiction is by definition fundamentally false, it offers a good venue for exposing unsupportable claims about the world. I like Russell's idea that a novelist provides an internal reality that is messier than history. I've been rereading *Les Misérables*—talk about messy! It certainly isn't the book I'd go to for an accurate account of French history, no more than I'd trust it on its claim about the nature of women. Yet it's thrilling to be suspended in its imagined world.

Lackey: Almost all biographical novels include a preface, an author's note, an afterword, or an epilogue, something as a disclaimer saying that this is just a work of fiction and it's not to be confused with biography or history. Why do you think so many biographical novelists feel this need to make this qualification? And why did you decide not to include such a statement in your work?
Scott: I thought it was obvious. It is called a novel so it is fiction. I would never want to say that it is "just" fiction. I don't like disclaimers. They are redundant and silly. It is a good thing they tend to be in very small font on the copyright page. Publishers put them in for legal purposes, I guess. But I would rather claim than disclaim. If I am calling a book fiction, if it is being presented as a novel, that should be enough.

Lackey: Shifting to the concept of the historical novel, Georg Lukács produced in the mid-thirties one of the most insightful and exhaustive studies of the historical novel. In that work, he argues that the biographical form of the novel is doomed to failure, because the focus on "the *biography of the hero*" lends authors to overlook or misrepresent significant historical events and truths. Given the nature of Lukács's critique, he would say that your novel is not just a failure. He would argue that it was doomed to failure from the outset, because the very form of the biographical novel is limited and even flawed. How would you respond to his critique?
Scott: I'm just glad Lukács is not around now to call me a failure. Worse than a failure! I would say, nothing is doomed to failure. If one hasn't written it, it could very well succeed.

Lackey: He would say it could succeed, but not as a historical novel.
Scott: Right, and only narrative methods associated with social realism are valid? Mann is good. Kafka is bad. I am all for widening the field, making it as inclusive as possible rather than restricting it. I know others find Lukács a useful guide. Nadine Gordimer has written persuasively about his importance. But if I understand the hypothetical situation here, a novel about a historical figure is doomed to failure because of its focus on the individual.

Lackey: His argument is that, because of the biographical novelist's invest-ment in and focus on a particular character, he or she is necessarily going to give us a distorted picture of history and the world. By centering the novel in a person's consciousness, the biographical novelist exaggerates a person's importance, so everything appears through a distorted lens.

Scott: Wasn't it the modernist immersion in individual subjectivity that Lukács was reacting against? I, as a late twentieth-century writer, was nur-tured by that immersion and it is absolutely what I love. I came to be a writer because I was reading Woolf and Faulkner and Conrad, all good dis-torters who remind us of the value of individual existence.

Lackey: But what can they give us in terms of understanding history that is different from and perhaps superior to the classical historical novel?

Scott: We've spoken about how any approach to history needs to consider the act of interpretation. Fiction writers spend a lot of time thinking about and showing us how we interpret the world. If we are going to think about how truth is constructed, then we need to get deep into the impressions of consciousness. I am certainly learning about experience when I am deep inside Benjy's mind in *Sound and Fury*, or deep inside Mrs. Dalloway's mind in *Mrs. Dalloway*.

Lackey: Or a biographical novel like Cunningham's *The Hours*?

Scott: Or *The Hours*, absolutely. Michael Cunningham gets us thinking about how we read the world, how we understand reality through the slant of personality. Writers can show us what is at stake in life without insisting that our existence becomes meaningful only when it is spread out on a vast scale. In terms of exploring what is involved in being human, a story about a single mind actively at work, responding to the world, can be as illuminating as a sprawling story of a famous battle.

Lackey: The mind is illuminated, but is history?

Scott: Even with an emphasis on the individual, maybe because of this emphasis, a fictional work set in the past can make us think about the reality of history. I go back to that mask of Napoleon again. We want to see what the person wearing the mask will do with it. But a good performance won't let us forget about Napoleon. The past may be distorted, but it is not erased in the kind of fiction we have been talking about. Even the most outlandish fiction—Barthelme's rendering of Cortes and Montezuma, for example—

will get us wondering about the past. I think that when it comes to art, there is more to learn from the act of distortion than from mimicry.

Lackey: Can you clarify the kind of truth you seek to represent in your novel *Arrogance*? More specifically, what is it that the biographical novel can communicate?

Scott: Well, here I would say that the phrase "biographical novel," as a category, makes me a bit nervous. I am nervous about all categories. They necessarily create restrictions. The challenge is to create the category but avoid relying on equations to define it. As soon as we have the equations, then the problem is solved. Unless, of course, the equations are wrong.

Lackey: I want to briefly address the ethics of a novel such as *Arrogance*. Even though your work is acknowledged to be a novel, is it possible that it infringes upon the rights of the subject under consideration? Can you talk about the ethical responsibility you have to Schiele and the other characters in the novel, that is, the obligation to represent their lives accurately? Also, can you define the kind of liberties you feel justified in taking with the facts? And can you specify the kind of liberties that you could not justify?

Scott: There is a lot packed into that question. In order to talk about ethics, I need to talk about precedence. Shortly before beginning *Arrogance*, I saw a beautiful production of Shakespeare's *King John* in London. In fact, I saw it twice. I wasn't thinking at the time of taking a major historical figure and fictionalizing him like Shakespeare did. But as a precedent, *King John* made very plain that there is a huge tradition of building fictions around historical characters. I was also familiar with Robert Coover's book *Public Burning*, which takes extraordinary liberties with Richard Nixon. Given these precedents, I don't think I hesitated at any point in taking some liberties and creating what seemed necessary in order to build this living, breathing thing we call a novel. I suppose the only kind of unjustifiable liberties would be the ones that don't contribute anything meaningful to the story.

Lackey: Can you discuss some scenes you created?

Scott: There are plenty of scenes in the novel that do not coincide with the biography. But I also took documented experiences and invented dialogue and thought to fill them in. There is a line in Grace Paley's "Conversations with my Father" in which the narrator says about a fictional character in a story she is writing, "she was my knowledge and my invention." Schiele was both my knowledge and my invention. I wanted to get my readers thinking about the limitations of my knowledge and the boundaries of the factual material, and at the same time to accept the invention on its own terms. One of the ways I tried to accomplish this was by opening each chapter with the comments of my narrator, who takes liberties with the life of Schiele. The best image I can use to describe my efforts in that novel is to point your attention to the scene in which the narrator as a girl is looking through the window at Schiele and Vallie sleeping. She can't possibly know what they are dreaming. But she can imagine. She creates her own versions of the two characters by watching them and then imagining what is happening in their minds as they are sleeping. Like her, I am standing outside of history, looking in through the window. I offer that scene as an example of my own relationship to the factual material that went into this novel.

Lackey: But we see her as an extremely flawed narrator. We don't trust her a whole lot.
Scott: Absolutely! She shouldn't be trusted.

Lackey: But I trust you more.
Scott: But you shouldn't! That is why it is a novel, don't trust me! Certainly don't count on me for accuracy. If my fellow novelist wants to get it right, as I said, I am going to get it wrong. Never trust a novelist.

Lackey: At one point in the novel the narrator says that "it is the artist's responsibility to educate" people's "eyes." Your novel is about an artist, and you spend considerable time clarifying how Schiele's art can educate our eyes. But what is it that the biographical novelist educates?
Scott: I've been learning what I can about the history of the novel since my own early years as a writer and have been aware of the somewhat fraught position that education has for novelists. Didacticism is something that has both energized the novel and has created terrible constraints for it, and many writers reacting against the didactic purposes of novels have created really interesting things in the name of self-expression. Yet it is a great thing when language educates, when art educates. Sitting here talking to you, I am being educated by your questions. We are educating ourselves through conversation about writing. I was and remain interested in trying to improve my understanding of experience. I learn from stories about mistakes. I like to read them and, if possible, write them. I like to write about how easily our impulsive responses can mislead us.

My young Schiele takes it upon himself to tell people what to think. He isn't always right, but he is often certain. There is some authorial ambivalence behind that comment about the artist's responsibility to educate. We need to be allowed the right to be impulsive if we are going to feel deeply, and we need to feel deeply if we are going to create worthy art. First impressions are valuable. On the other hand, we can easily misjudge things that are unfamiliar. And when we make art, the work is easily botched if we rely only on impulse. The Schiele in *Arrogance* is not always the best teacher. And yet he recognizes that if we want to give a full experience of art, we need to act boldly, without worrying about pleasing the audience.

Does this make sense? I'm trying to unknot the ambivalence behind the claim that the artist teaches people how to look at the world. I believe it, and I don't believe it. I wanted to spur readers to recognize the usefulness and dangers of impulsiveness. Schiele, as I have drawn him, is an impulsive artist. His passion is productive and gives him fierce insights. But the same passion can make him unwaveringly certain about the legitimacy of his views. So when he lectures about the importance of the artist, I am hoping there is a note of caution ringing softly in the background.

Lackey: Something in the nature of the biographical novel is inherently multidisciplinary. As a biographical novelist of Schiele's life you must have a commanding grasp of Viennese Secessionist art, Austrian history, Schiele's biography, and European politics, etc. Can you discuss both the challenge and value of the biographical novel in giving readers a multidisciplinary picture of character and history?
Scott: Well, there we go. This is the answer to Lukács: The biographical novel is multidisciplinary, varied, mosaic—as vast as those big sprawling novels by Mann and Balzac—which I do love, I have to add. So maybe my efforts aren't doomed to failure.

No, I do not claim expertise, I never did. I am trying to express fascination with my subject. The period known as the *fin de siècle* in Vienna was very fruitful. It deserves to be pondered, and it is exciting to explore. As a novelist, I can share my enthusiasm. I can give my own version of a tour through the period. I can say to my readers, "Come with me. Take this trip, so come along with me and let's see what we see." But I am no expert. I have always insisted that as a novelist I am not an expert. If I have any expertise, it is with the basic material of fictional language. By this point in my life, I should be able to say something useful about the arrangement of words in a work of imaginative prose. But I will leave history to the historians and thank them for the groundwork that they have done.

You ask about the challenge of the biographical novel. The challenge follows very clearly from this discussion of expertise. If one doesn't have expertise, then there are areas of ignorance that are profound. That is part of the package; to me that is true of any novel I have written and will ever write, whether it is about Vienna at the turn of the twentieth century or the street in Connecticut where I grew up. There are a lot of things I will never know. Even within the mind of a single invented character, there are a lot of things I don't know. The individual is so complex, fictional or biographical. And then the time period, any time period, is *so* complex. Trying to honor the complex beauty of an individual, a place, a time, without knowing everything—that is the challenge. But if we only took on subjects about which we have absolute knowledge, we wouldn't have fiction, or any art. So much of the pleasure I get from art is in understanding what the artist has done with her subject. It is not the accuracy of the representation that concerns me. It is the way the artist works with the subject. To watch the artist in action, working on or responding to something—I learn from that, I learn about what we can do and what we can think and what we haven't thought before. Every new sentence teaches me something new about the potential of the mind.

Lackey: You are working on a biographical novel right now. Can you talk about the differences between dealing with somebody like Egon Schiele and the person you are working on now?

Scott: My main subject in this new book is a man named Armand de Potter, who ran a travel business in the late nineteenth century and led tours through Europe and around the world. While he was doing this, he also was assembling a notable collection of ancient Egyptian art. He died mysteriously at sea in 1905. The book tells the story of that mystery and is an attempt to solve it drawing from archival materials that have turned up in my family. I started working on this book after I discovered a set of diaries that his widow left behind when she died. All the challenges we've been talking about, and the values associated with biography and fiction, or history and fiction, seem really relevant to me now. There is an added challenge in that this figure is my ancestor and has been somewhere in my imagination since I was a child. I heard stories about him for years and had wondered what happened. I was told that he disappeared at sea. What does that mean, to disappear at sea? This figure, this ancestor, came alive to me when I started to read my great-grandmother's diaries. But still it is very challenging to work with him, to take him out of history, out of the factual swamp, and to reinvent him as a fictional character. It is exciting but difficult.

Lackey: And how is it difficult in a different way from the Schiele novel?
Scott: I think because I am older. I was young and reckless when I wrote *Arrogance*. I am far more mature.

Lackey: Were you arrogant?
Scott: I was! The original title of that book was *Travels and Confessions of a Pair of Shoes*. Don't ask me to explain that! Then it changed to *Travels and Confessions of a Wunderkind* and then it changed to *Arrogance* at the end. I found myself thinking about the arrogance of Schiele himself, the arrogance of the audience, and my own arrogance as a twenty-eight-year-old American woman taking on this material and trying to make it my own. I think I am probably more cautious now in treating the factual material than I was, even though I still insist that what is important is the invention. The other thing is that even though there wasn't a whole lot of material available about Schiele—that had been translated into English at least—there was enough. And the subject I am working on now—there is a ton of material, volumes and volumes of diaries, letters, legal documents, but it is not enough. So the ground is a little bit more precarious for this new project, which is part of the fun.

Lackey: To conclude, could you identify some of the best biographical novels being written today? And could you explain why they are, in your estimation, some of the best?
Scott: Well, since early on, I have been interested in the way representations of history can mix with the expressions of fiction. Earlier this week I found myself opening up Angela Carter's book of stories *Saints and Strangers* and rereading her "Fall River Ax Murders," which is about Lizzie Borden. I saw that I marked it up with comments. I must have reread it several times when I was younger. She works with history in other ways throughout that collection. I found her explorations exciting when I was a young writer. She was a freeing kind of influence for me. So I cite her as a really fine example of the kinds of mixing we have been talking about. Thinking back over the past thirty years, I can track other influences. When I was just out of college and trying to learn how to be a writer, I had the opportunity to read Salman Rushdie's *Shame* in manuscript. I was enthralled by his brazen interruptions in the story, when the narrator stops a fictional scene to explain the sources he used to create his fictional characters. Another writer who

has done some of the most interesting work in these terms is Sebald. He includes visual material to create a really provocative relationship between facts and fiction. It is very exciting work, I think. Michael Cunningham has managed to mix history and fiction in innovative ways. Parini and Banks are able to absorb us beautifully in their re-creations and revisions of history. I am intrigued by John Coetzee's fictional version of John Coetzee. Also, I have come to love the collage of quotations in David Markson's late novels. Somehow he makes a moving fictional narrative out of other writers' words. I am drawn to any art that offers evidence of ingenuity without seeming self-congratulatory. I like to see fiction tested and expanded so that the genre itself becomes freshly relevant. Really, I am looking for anything that introduces me to an idiosyncratic way of thinking and at the same gives insight into the expressive potential of language.

An Interview with Joanna Scott

Martin Naparsteck / 2015

Previously unpublished. Reprinted by permission of Martin Naparsteck.

Joanna Scott has published eight novels and two collections of short stories. Her 1996 novel, *The Manikin*, was a finalist for the Pulitzer Prize. *Arrogance* (a novel, 1990) and *Various Antidotes* (stories, 1994) were both nominees for the PEN/Faulkner Award. Her stories have appeared in both *The Best American Stories* and *The Pushcart Prize*. Her new novel, *De Potter's Grand Tour*, is forthcoming from Farrar, Straus, and Giroux.

She has received both MacArthur and Guggenheim fellowships and the Rosenthal Award from the American Academy of Arts and Letters. Scott teaches at the University of Rochester.

Martin Naparsteck: In what ways, if any, do you write differently today than when you first started to write a few decades ago? Faster, slower? Do you think what is good writing today is different than what you thought was good writing, say, twenty years ago? Is writing today easier or harder? More fun or less fun? Are there differences that surprise you?

Joanna Scott: I still remember beginning the first manic sentence of my first novel—"I will tell you exactly how it was one day I said." I wrote it in a rage, after I'd been a student for just a few months too long—I was fed up with being told how to write, and it was my turn to do the telling. I wrote it with a sense of urgency—who could say how much time we will be allotted on earth? I was also laughing as I wrote—laughing at the potential for nonsense offered by the blank page. Actually, it wasn't entirely a blank page. It was a lined page in a notebook, and I was writing by freehand. So this tells me something, in hindsight. I could write anything. And yet I had to keep my letters sandwiched between the lines. You'd think that twenty—more like thirty years later—I'd be more aware of the implications of the initial choices a writer must make, more attuned to the nuances of language, more cautious as I add words to a sentence. But I still believe in the virtue of spontaneity. I still look with bafflement at the empty page, my pulse starts to race, I say to myself, this time I'm going to get it right. As far as I can tell, I'm just as hopeful as I was when I was twenty-four. I'm still left-handed. But I've broken the pinky on my left hand twice—that changes something, I guess. And my appreciation of good writing keeps changing with my evolving interests as a reader.

Naparsteck: How did you break your finger?
Scott: I was holding the reins too loosely when I went over a jump on a horse. The horse hesitated at the base then took a big, round leap over the rail, and I bumped my hand hard against his neck (the horse was oblivious) and shattered my finger. Then, because I'm me, I did the same stupid thing again a few years later.

Naparsteck: Is the bafflement you refer to, the bafflement you see when you look at the blank screen, useful (perhaps it forces you to think of things you might not otherwise think of), a hindrance, just something you've learned to live with, or something I'm not listing?
Scott: It's more than useful—bafflement is the necessary preface to the choices we have to make if we're going to create something new out of sentences. It's hard enough to explain what we think we already know, to choose the best words and arrange them in persuasive order. Writing fiction is of a different order. When I sit down and try to conjure a story out of airy nothing, I'm aware, maybe too aware these days, of the multitude of possibilities. That said, I would go mad if I just kept weighing one potential phrase against another. I don't let myself worry too much about impact— that can be addressed in revision. Instead, I try to preserve a devil-may-care attitude when I begin writing. I remain comfortable discarding false starts. I still trust that weird impulse we call instinct and am always waiting for that moment when I feel things click into place.

Naparsteck: When you say you are "comfortable discarding false starts" are you talking about starting on a story or a novel, or were you talking about starting every scene, or maybe every paragraph?
Scott: I'm referring to the challenge of starting any new project, a story or a novel. I'm no stranger to the experience of writing deeply into something and realizing that it's not viable. I can move on without too much agony. I'm also more willing to try and rehaul a work of fiction.

Naparsteck: Was there a time early on that you might have felt that you wrote something that was so sacred that you weren't allowed to discard it?

Scott: I'm nervous about applying the word "sacred" to any work of fiction. It's true that I used to be in more of a hurry. I kept wanting to get to the end, but now I really like being in the middle of something. I also am taking new pleasure in the backward work of revision.

Naparsteck: When you discard a false start, do you ever go back to it, months later, years later?

Scott: I'm not too careful about keeping my files neat, which has been a problem in my life. "Out of sight, out of mind" is a good way to clean the house, as far as I'm concerned. But I do go through those messy files once in a while. I've drawn from old material and reinvigorated a stalling story. Generally, though, I like to leave behind my past work and surge forward and enjoy the freshness of discovery.

Naparsteck: At what point in a story do you have a sense that you know what the ending is going to be?

Scott: That varies. I'm comfortable with more ambiguity at the end of stories. The neatness of a tight ending tends to dissatisfy me both as a reader and a writer. With novels I suppose I have a clearer sense of the general arc of something and am more willing to draw loose ends together in some fashion. I found myself thinking hard about direction—the direction of the narrative, the direction of Sally Werner's life—while writing *Follow Me*. As the author, I could do what my characters were doing—I could wander off track, I could skip ahead or circle back or even stumble and stutter and obfuscate, as long as I kept the final destination in mind.

Naparsteck: Despite that sense of wandering, do you reach a point where there's a sense of inevitability?

Scott: I love that tug of inevitability. We've been talking a lot about the possibilities available to a writer of fiction, and I really want to honor that. But a sentence needs to follow from its subject to make sense. Then that sentence expands into a scene and the scene expands into a chapter. The portion of a narrative that is already written necessarily influences and restricts the wandering that follows.

Naparsteck: Is the inevitability a result, or the product maybe, of what you think, as you start to develop a character? Perhaps you think this is what this guy has to do, or is it something in you?

Scott: I think more about the logic or pattern of thought rather than about actions in the plot. Ways of thinking define a character. I try to remain true to the pattern. At the same time, I am always trying to attend to the complexity of that personality and capture the inconsistencies.

Naparsteck: Do you ever find yourself in conflict with the character, that they want to do one thing and you want them to do another?

Scott: (Laughing) Oh, they always do what I tell them to do. No, that's not true. A character can surprise me or I can surprise myself in what I didn't perceive as possible. I like to talk with my students about Elizabeth Bishop's idea for revision. She once suggested that if you reach a point in writing when you think something isn't working—more precisely, if you are stuck on a problematic word—try changing that word to its opposite. Change "yes" to "no," "stop" to "go." I'm probably misrepresenting Bishop here— I don't think she was as methodological about this as I'm suggesting. But I like the counterintuitive aspect of the advice and have found it a useful strategy—one strategy among many.

Naparsteck: Having read recently a book called *Contested Will* by James Shapiro, where he argues that the people who say Shakespeare didn't write Shakespeare are wrong—one of the points he makes is that the people who argue that simply underestimate the power of imagination, that, for example, you don't really have to be part of the queen's court to understand what goes on in the queen's court enough to write about it. I do get the impression in reading your work that you do have a lot of faith in the power of imagination. Could you talk a little about that? It seems to me that so many young writers today think that as a starting point you have to write about yourself, about your life experiences.

Scott: The very fact that we're beginning a story that is by definition not true means that we have to leave ourselves behind to some extent. For some writers it's not a great extent, for other writers it is, and the effort goes more toward imagining than remembering. I'm always puzzling over exactly what imagination is. I've built a course around this question [at the University of Rochester] and am trying to explore the evolution of theories of imagination, from Plato and Aristotle to Sartre and Mary Warnock and Elaine Scarry. All these theorists of the imagination ask us to stop and think about what is really happening when we're making mental images. What are we doing when we're imagining something, what's going on in our brain? What's going on when we try to create mental images verbally for the reader? And how does the imagined thing affect us emotionally? There's always a little bit of danger in imagining—if we let ourselves go too far, you know, if the fantasy becomes real, then we're in the realm of psychosis. Fiction has a foot in that realm—maybe more than a foot.

Naparsteck: Some writers talk about role playing like an actor and acting out the character. Do you find yourself doing anything like that?
Scott: Tell me a little more about that.

Naparsteck: Well, if you're writing about a murderer and you're going to stab someone in the back, you might actually pick up a knife—if you find a volunteer. Of course, it probably wouldn't be murder then.
Scott: Yeah, yeah. That's not a good idea, that kind of role modeling. Especially for some of the characters I create. One of my distinct goals is to stir sympathy in a reader. I don't really believe in the necessity of identifying with the character, to see one's life mirrored in the fiction. It's more important to feel what it's like, temporarily, to be someone else, to have to face something that a character is facing—that's one of the deepest satisfactions fiction can offer. Thanks to my modern lit class this semester, I'm discovering the great rush of sympathy in books I thought I already knew. Faulkner and Woolf, James and Conrad—they all give us a chance to experience different ways of being in the world. But to get back to your question, to what extent does role playing or acting out the character help in writing? I guess I do think theatrically. I like to imagine fiction on a stage, to picture something—talking about the mental image—as if it were lit up by the artificial light of a theater. I can't explain why this is useful to me, but it suggests that acting out is exactly what I'm doing. I'm taking time to arrange this bundle of words into something that is then performed by a character. I often read aloud in order to get a better sense of the rhythm of a voice. I don't worry about actually turning into my characters.

Naparsteck: To whatever extent you do that, could you find within yourself some emotion that, say, that I really am capable, not of murdering someone, but of hating somebody or of being jealous of people I shouldn't be jealous of, of having negative emotions.
Scott: (Laughs) Gosh, you're going deep here. This is scary territory. I don't know. In writing a violent scene, my sympathy of course is going to the victim. But I'm always trying to figure out motivation, so I turn my attention to the perpetrator and try to understand what's driving him or her. Whether

thinking about that then leads me to want to turn the fiction into some experiential reality, I don't think I go quite that far in my life.

Naparsteck: Are you aware of the working methods of other writers that you admire: do they do things like that? For example, some writers seem heavily autobiographical. Richard Yates comes to mind. Some writers seem, if not all that autobiographical, still to be part of what's going on in their writing. Mark Twain comes to mind. Are you aware of thinking, maybe I should be finding out what this one guy did, how he wrote.

Scott: I'm thinking about the work of other writers all the time. I've been spending a lot of time these past few weeks thinking hard about Joyce's *A Portrait of the Artist as a Young Man*. It's a book that I've always admired but it resisted me. This time round I've come to understand it in a new way. I always located the culmination of the book with the journal entries at the end. Now it seems to me that it comes just before Stephen is about to launch into first-person, when he's walking with his friend Cranly and he suddenly recognizes Cranly's loneliness. I've missed the importance of this scene in past readings. It's an example of how I will keep thinking about a book. I will take it apart in the way a mechanic will take apart a car, and maybe at a certain point I will reach an understanding that satisfies me. Also, I spent time over the summer revisiting *Ulysses* and trying to hear it in a new way, and that's been very helpful. I take apart the book, as I said, as the mechanic might take apart the car. I tend not to take apart the writer's life. I love stories, and biographies are full of stories. But if we want to learn how to write fiction, it's better to read the work itself than a biography of the writer. Anyway, I don't fully trust biographies. I really don't trust autobiographies. I don't trust writers when they give interviews. Maybe you shouldn't trust me now.

Naparsteck: Can you sense when you're reading a novel or short story that this must be autobiographical, or you just don't know? Or would you rather not know?

Scott: No. I've recently written about the experience of reading *The Sound and the Fury* for the first time when I was a teenager. I had no idea in later years that that book had such a huge influence on me as a young writer. I was oblivious that Faulkner was behind all the echoes and pale imitations I attempted. But what matters to me are the words that make up *The Sound and the Fury*. Faulkner lived a colorful life, and so that's fascinating in itself. But it's his arrangement of words on the page that matters, not his drinking habits.

Naparsteck: Which writers are you aware of influencing your writing? Specifically, not teachers, not people who have taught you. In addition to Faulkner, who do you think that by reading them have influenced the way you've written? And also, can some writers be bad influences?

Scott: At my age it's useful to think about how influence changes over the years—the influence of Faulkner or Woolf, Beckett or Dickens, as I reread and reabsorb their work. I am just rereading Gertrude Stein's *The Autobiography of Alice B. Toklas.* I love the way the trick of it becomes so much a part of the texture, the language. The ironies are really delicious in that book. Nabokov might be a good example of a bad influence. He's one of my favorites. But every time I find myself thinking about Nabokov when I'm writing, the results are awful. It will be a false start, I can guarantee you.

Naparsteck: Nabokov, Dickens, Faulkner are big names. Are there writers less well known that might influence you?

Scott: Well, sure. These include my colleagues, people close to me, writers I exchange work with. There are Maureen Howard and Steve Erickson. When I was a young writer I met Angela Carter, and her extravagances really appealed to me. I feel nurtured by friendships—Rikki Ducornet, Brad Morrow, Mary Caponegro, Bruce Bauman. I love every word Stephen Millhauser writes. I like discovering new passions by reading for prizes and reviewing—Dagoberto Gilb, Edith Pearlman, Nicole Krauss, Edward P. Jones—I find their work nurturing. I am married to a poet and so am treated to lots of contact with poets. Our schedule revolves around visiting poets. When the phone rings in our house, it's usually a poet calling.

Naparsteck: When did you first start reading a lot?

Scott: There was a bit of idealization of reading in my family when I was young, so we were all supposed to be reading. But in fact we didn't have a whole lot of books in the house, and so we were more apt to be playing football—me too—than to be reading. Yet the process certainly developed when I was young. Reading is a process that we need to keep cultivating and developing. We need to keep learning how to do it. We can settle into the sturdy security of sophistication a little too easily, I think, and miss some important work that's out there. I would hope that what I've been doing all my life is becoming a better reader.

Naparsteck: I think I learned to read twice: once as a kid and again when I finished graduate school.

Scott: And then again as a teacher, and as a writer. And then as a reviewer. And writing essays.

Naparsteck: Can you tell me something about your personal writing habits? Do you write every day? Do you have a certain time to write? Can you write any time you want to? Do deadlines help you?
Scott: You know, life is so complicated, so many responsibilities and interruptions and if it's not the dog that needs to be walked, it's papers needing to be graded. So these days I'm much more scattered than I've ever been in my life. I don't know when I write any more. (Laughs) Am I still writing? It's hard trying to make all the pieces fit together.

Naparsteck: Regardless of whether or not you have interruptions, has your total output changed or is it still pretty much the same?
Scott: I don't know. I guess it has changed. I've been working on one book for a longer period lately, a book that uses a lot of archival material. I've been having fun slowly working through some of the challenges of the project, though there have been points when I despair that I'll never get it done.

Naparsteck: Talking about having fun, is there any relationship between how much fun you have writing something and how good you think it is?
Scott: Oh, I hope there is because I want to have fun. And so I hope that success is related to that. I think that it is. There's also satisfaction that comes when something is really difficult. I have faced some very difficult challenges with this new project as I try to negotiate all the historical material.

Naparsteck: What is this one?
Scott: It's a novel called *The Gilt Cabinet*.[1] It's based on material that turned up unexpectedly in our family. Diaries and journals and photographs and prints, lantern slides, old legal documents. Boxes and boxes of stuff that had been forgotten and stuck in attics and basements and the back of my mother's closet. I combed through it all a few years ago and discovered that the material in those boxes solved—or mostly solved—a mystery that had been passed along through generations in my family. The story involves my mother's grandfather, who in 1905 disappeared at sea. He made his living leading tours around the world, and he also collected Egyptian antiquities. No one saw him go overboard, and his body was never found. The story of his mysterious disappearance was passed along through the generations. And then I discovered that at least part of the explanation had been passed along, as well.

Naparsteck: I think most of your work, maybe all of it, seems to involve a good deal of research. Do you feel an obligation, if you're researching history, to get the history right, or—clearly you can make up some things—but if there's something historical that could happen, could you—

Scott: It's always a good question, and always something that I do ask myself. I never come up with a good answer. I love to play around. Fiction is about play. Play is essential for the art of fiction. If fiction is drawing from history, then history needs to be available for play. Little kids play with history and make new things happen. But, then, I'm not interested in revising history. I guess the main reason I am looking back at the past is to discover the stories that have been lost. And since they're lost, one way I can discover them is to make them up. And then the other reason I like to look back, almost as important, but not quite, is to help us avoid making the same mistakes twice.

Naparsteck: In doing the research do you ever feel frustrated that the proof you want that something happened just isn't available to you, perhaps because you can't find the right documents, and could you also feel frustrated that you're creating a character who just turns out to be somebody else?

Scott: I guess that's one of the challenges I'm facing now. I'm looking for the absolute proof of something, and life doesn't usually give us absolutes.

Naparsteck: Do you ever see yourself writing a nonfiction book? You write nonfiction articles.

Scott: Yeah, absolutely. I love doing two kinds of essays. One, meditations on a theme, on a general subject. And then I do really welcome the chance to write at length about work I think is important to our culture.

Naparsteck: How conscious are you of your style as you're writing? Is it something that comes naturally, or do you ever consciously try to change your style, and, if so, are you successful when you try to change it?

Scott: That's a really good question. I like to hear other writers speak about this. Once a few years back I had to put my signature on multiple sheets of transparent velum, and with each sheet I tried to change my signature, to make it bigger and smaller, longer, shorter. But when I put all the pieces of velum together in a pile, I could see that the signature was exactly the same. So this tells me that I'm not going to be changing my style. As much as possible, though, I want to extend whatever inherent style I have, to shape it in accordance with the requirements of a particular book, a character's sensibility, to make the sentences match the fictional sensibility.

Naparsteck: If you didn't know what you had written, and if you took your first one, two, or three books and compared the style to the last one, two, or three books, do you think you would be able to notice the difference?
Scott: I forgot to use paragraphs when I wrote my first novel. My editor told me I needed paragraphs, so I put in paragraphs. I use lots of paragraphs now.

Naparsteck: When do you find writing either the hardest or the easiest? Is it easier to describe the physical appearance of a character or easier to get the dialogue right?
Scott: I have always appreciated the power of fiction to make us responsive, not just to get us absorbed imaginatively, but then to give us the ability to go out and see the world with a freshness and intensity. This often translates for me into enthusiasm for visual description. Conrad has that famous preface: the task of the writer, he says, is to make the reader hear, to make you feel, above all, to make you see. I still feel great pleasure when I'm using language that is visually oriented. And then when I'm reading it, too.

Naparsteck: Why did you become a writer? Instead of, say, a football player? You said you played football.
Scott: I still play football now and then. We just pumped up our deflated football yesterday. Writing is something I knew I would always do. Call it a fixation. It was there. It was going to be part of my life for better or for worse. Maybe it's for worse sometimes; I don't know (laughs). I don't worry about defining myself as a writer, and I'm not even sure I do that now. I remember my teacher, Jack Hawkes, saying, "Don't call me a writer; I write." Writing is something active and constantly changing. But I hardly had the chance to make the choice. It just happened. My curse at birth.

Martin Naparsteck has published two novels, *War Song* and *A Hero's Welcome*; a collection of short stories, *Saying Things*; a book of writing advice, *Honesty in the Use of Words*; and a critical study, *Richard Yates Up Close*. His latest book is a work of history, *Sex and Manifest Destiny*.

Notes

1. Retitled *De Potter's Grand Tour*.

An Interview with Joanna Scott

Bruce Bauman / 2017

From *Slice Magazine*, no. 21 (2017): 16–21. Reprinted by permission of Bruce Bauman.

I met Joanna Scott about twenty years ago when I'd read two of her novels, which had entranced me. And her books have continued to do so ever since. I remain in awe of her ability to transcend form and genre. In some ways she reminds me of Iris Murdoch in the manner in which she delves into the motivations and contradictions of good and evil, exploring the human condition, writing philosophical and politically inspired works that are riveting—and giving us another terrific novel every two or three years. Her newest book, *Careers for Women*, is my current favorite. That's sort of like picking a favorite Beatles song: it changes with my mood. But damn, this book is special. I'm not alone in singing her praises: Scott has won a MacArthur Foundation Fellowship, a Guggenheim Fellowship, and a Lannan Foundation award for fiction, and her books have been finalists for the Pulitzer Prize, the PEN/Faulkner Award, and the *Los Angeles Times* Book Prize.

Bruce Bauman: Since your novels cannot be easily categorized, I wonder how you pick your subjects—or do they pick you? For example, how did you decide to write about Schiele thirty years ago, a taxidermist in upstate New York twenty years ago, and now women working in public relations in the fifties, sixties, and seventies?

Joanna Scott: I guess I can say I pick the subjects that pick me. They pick me just by catching my eye, often when my focus is elsewhere. I settle on the ones that promise to sustain my attention and give me something new to learn. I'm always on the lookout for anything whose relevance is hidden or unexpected. Schiele, taxidermy, the PR department at the Port Authority—they all struck me as relevant in surprising ways.

BB: In *Careers for Women*, Lee Jaffe is not the narrator of the novel but is its catalytic character. Jaffe (like Schiele) was a real person, who served as the New York City Port Authority's director of public relations from 1944 to 1965, and despite my wonderful NYC public school education, I had never heard of her. How did she pick you?

JS: We don't know much about the real Lee Jaffe, but it's clear that she was a business leader with a visionary sense of the city's potential. She made her way into my imagination after I came across a brief reference to her in one of the old newspapers I'd saved from autumn 2001. In 1960, she penned a somewhat whimsical memo in which she challenged the executives at the Port Authority to build the tallest building in the world to house the World Trade Center. Maybe if she hadn't written that memo, different sorts of structures would have been built, and history might have taken a different turn. In my fictional version of her, I wanted to emphasize her strength and vision, and at the same time to honor the basic fact that we can't know the future and can only guess at the consequences of our best intentions.

BB: In the portrayal by Maggie, the narrator of the novel, Mrs. J (Jaffe) is a no-bullshit-taking mother superior, who is as tough as she is well intentioned. (She kind of reminded me of my mom, who started as a receptionist at an ad agency in the sixties and ended up a VP; she always hired women when she could, but she also always knew that many of her bosses—all men—were unscrupulous and always in charge.) Although it's the direct and indirect actions of one man, Bob Whittaker, that cause so much of the pain, the women in the novel are betrayed, abused, and abandoned by the men in their lives despite Jaffe's good intentions. And yet—and I marvel at how you achieved this—it doesn't feel like a rant or an angry book. It seethes, and it's heartbreaking at times, yet Maggie's narration gives it a magnificent charm, warmth, and generosity.

JS: Your mom sounds like a visionary pioneer in her own right!

BB: She was and would've told you that.

JS: It couldn't have been easy for her.

BB: She would've told you that too.

JS: You really capture the feelings I was experiencing at my desk as I imagined these different characters in action. As I see it, there is just one prodigious villain in the book, and that is Bob Whittaker—much of what you allude to happens because of him. With his portrait, I set out to trace how violence can result from a slow-burning corruption, a way of thinking that involves weird, contorted logic. In his effort to justify himself, Bob becomes increasingly confused. I put his stepson, Robbie, in a position that is meant to offer sharp contrast. As for the pressures that Jaffe and Maggie have to endure, they were endemic in the business culture at the time. My own childhood was certainly touched, if not shaped, by the postwar gender dynamic (in my family's case, the old order went topsy-turvy when my father became unemployable and my mother found a job). But it's not just that I'm trying to capture a period sentiment; as in all my books, from my first novel on, I've been trying to examine the ways misogyny provokes action in a wide variety of forms—dominance, bluster, violence on one side; stealthy resistance, submission, revolt, camaraderie on the other.

BB: That raises the question of feminism and how you subtly portray it as both a politically and socially charged subject. Your books are not often overtly political, but they often deal with relationships that have larger implications in the cultural and political realms. Do you agree with that? If so, how does that fit into your role as an artist?

JS: Like most people, I boil with passionate indignation and rage at the tragedy and injustice in the world. And like most writers, I let those feelings infuse my fiction. But I am also motivated by more deliberate ambitions. I want to understand what drives a person to cause harm . . . thus my interest in inhabiting the minds of egotists, bigots, villains.

BB: [Badly singing] "Egotist, bigot, villain, president, oh my . . ." Do you see any link between the themes of your book and the rise of Trump and the defeat of Clinton? Is Clinton a sort of Jaffe-like figure?

JS: I finished the preliminary draft of the novel before the campaign heated up, but I like the connection you propose. And of course it would be impossible to create a portrait of a powerful woman without thinking of Clinton. Don't get me going—a woman of great strength, experience, and dignity was subjected to the vilest insults ever launched in a public campaign. But far more concerning than Trump's attacks was the rabid mob mentality of the audience. At least we have a good, clear record of it all. Those chants of "lock her up" will echo for generations to come. Years from now, we will be looking at the videos of Trump delivering that shout-out to the "Second Amendment people." Thanks to the historical record, we will remember how

Trump's supporters cheered him on. And thanks to fiction, we can break up the mob into individuals and expose the private thinking that feeds zealotry.

BB: Speaking of that cross between historical reality and fiction, the World Trade Center seems to be appearing in lots of books these days: Steve Erickson uses the towers in a completely different way in *Shadowbahn*. You've given us a history of them of which I, and I think most people, were unaware. How do you see the WTC as a symbol of the past and future of America?

JS: I remember a powerful glimpse of the towers in your most recent novel.

BB: Thanks.

JS: And I was fascinated to see those ghostly towers rising in Steve's futuristic rendering. In my case, I don't mean for them to figure symbolically. I'm trying to show how because of them, a partnership is created between a small upstate community and New York City; the contract between the aluminum company and the Port Authority binds the rural and urban economies, and it ends up reconnecting Pauline and Bob Whittaker. If there's any symbol floating around the book, it's aluminum. What an interesting metal, so useful and abundant, yet take one look at those aluminum plants upstate and you can see that workable aluminum comes to us at great cost.

BB: I could see Trump's face as the symbol of Alumacore, the company you created in the book, which is essential to the plot but also feels symbolic. Jaffe's monumental vision is in part brought down not just by terrorists but perhaps by the corrupt practices of Alumacore. Hillary built something that was monumental—or would've been, but it was destroyed by a political terrorist like Trump at a great cost to America. This makes the book, to me, especially timely without being overtly political.

JS: I don't think I'm the best one to explain how this novel about the past might connect to the present, but absolutely, my concerns about our fragile world find expression in my fiction. In some ways, it's hard to recover exactly what was in my head while I was composing this book. I wrote the bulk of it rapidly, during a period of intense isolation in Marfa, Texas. I sat down at a desk, opened my computer, and fell into a trance. Twenty-eight days later, I had the first draft of the novel completed. I've never written anything in this way before, with such unbroken concentration. I was a hermit in the desert, and the concept of the novel presented itself to me as a problem I needed to solve before I did anything else. I had the solution, but it unfolded so fast, I could hardly keep up with it. Of course, when I came back to earth and reread what I'd written, I saw that the pages were rough and needed reworking. It was during the long process of revision that I could think more decisively about meaning and make adjustments to sharpen the implications.

BB: Okay, so you wrote the first draft at Marfa, but much of it takes place in rural New York (as have other of your novels). I've driven through those towns, almost ghost towns, once thriving and now grim, in New York and western Massachusetts and Connecticut. I think you really captured the feel of those places in your creation of Visby, where Alumacore has a plant. Did you do much research on these towns? Travel to them?

JS: I've lived in western New York for most of my adult life and have traveled in all corners of the state, but this is the first time I've gone so far north for a fictional setting. I had a haunting experience when I went to do some research at the Akwesasne library in Hogansburg. I wasn't sure what I was looking for and was just browsing. I was about to leave when I stumbled on a shelf full of old reports about the environmental devastation caused by the aluminum industry. These gave me key pieces of information. But I was also struck by the beauty of the region and its rich history. I've set other books in different upstate areas, and I'm always trying to show the flip side to that grimness you mention. The factories may have left scars, but the land is fertile, fresh water is abundant, and the rhythm of four distinct seasons keeps life exciting.

BB: You seem to find optimism in some very dark places in your books. This quote seemed like one of the direst: Cy, the retired high school social studies teacher, gives a little lecture about history and the Alumacore fire, and it ends, "But we have never figured out how to learn from our mistakes, now, have we?" Do you agree with that? Is that a subtle message of this book?

JS: It's interesting to see you pick out that line. It was added very late in revision—a result of one of those adjustments I mentioned. Now that I think about it, maybe it came out of my despair at the ugliness exposed in the election. But here's the thing: I've lived long enough to feel frustrated with my natural tendency toward pessimism, so I've decided to be an optimist and see what happens. Didn't it all work out for Candide in the long run? Maybe in the future we will figure out how to learn from our mistakes. Who knows, maybe our struggling genre of fiction will help light the way.

BB: I see not only the genre of fiction struggling, but language in general. In 1946, George Orwell wrote "Politics and the English Language," in which he proclaims that the English language is "in a bad way." He also wrote, "Now, it is clear that the decline of a language must ultimately have political and economic causes." My questions: Do you think the American language is in a bad way? Does the decline of language precede political and economic disarray, or is it the other way around?

JS: These may be the central questions for writers in our time—or in any time. We know that languages tend to change, sometimes gradually, sometimes abruptly. New words come in, unused idioms go out. English has been particularly flexible and open to influence, mostly to enriching effect. But I do share the chilling impression that literacy has entered a crisis period, and we are losing the gains we've made in the last century. Consider the warning signs: The portion of nonreaders in this country has risen dramatically in two decades. The number of American adults who read no books at all in a year has almost tripled since the 1970s. The whole mission of the humanities is under siege. Reading literature has become a form of rarified study—only snowflakes do it.

It just so happens that I've been poring over George Steiner's essay on translation—he warns that there are times when words go dead, when syntax stiffens and "the available resources of live perception and restatement wither." I fear that's exactly what we're facing. Our available resources are withering . . . though I wouldn't say it's because of some comical mangling at the top of the food chain. I think the problem is a conniving embrace of illiteracy. Ideas are communicated in monosyllabic shorthand, with words like *rigged, fake, sad* used as clever obfuscation. It's a strategy aimed at convincing people that they don't need to read because they don't need to think.

I should point out that Steiner didn't share Orwell's pessimism about language. In that same essay, Steiner celebrates the "acquisitive brilliance" of American English—this was back in the late 1970s, when the language was looking more robust. Isn't this exactly the historical contrast you go after in your own books, as you trace how art and language are broken?

BB: Yes, that was one of my aims in both novels, and my answer would be complex—especially when it comes to obfuscations and silences as lies. I will add that social media and what I called "speedfeed news" in *Broken Sleep* are pieces of that breakdown. What do you think are the short- and long-term repercussions of social media?

JS: At best, social media offers a forum for legitimate organizing, advocacy, and self-expression; at worst, it is an unrestricted field for propaganda. Between those extremes, it seems to provide mildly entertaining opportunities for procrastination. I do think it's important to start working with children early on to help them develop critical skills, so they won't be overwhelmed by the bunkum.

BB: Well, there sure is whole lotta bunkum floating around. How does that—what this profane person might call *bullshit*—inspire your work?
JS: Well, Profane Person, I'll suggest that there's a difference—bunkum is associated with nonsense and excess, bullshit with outright fraud. So how does bullshit inspire? There's no beauty without contrast. Take a good, stinking dose of something ugly, mix it with its opposite, and stir. That's one recipe for making something beautiful and lasting.

Interview with Joanna Scott

Lisa Tschernkowitsch / 2017

Interview conducted on Wednesday, September 26, 2017, for WCBS Author Talks podcast, Chapter 31. Reprinted by permission.

Lisa Tschernkowitsch: In her book *Careers for Women,* author Joanna Scott turns a little-known New York City public figure into a central character. That person is Lee Jaffe, the former head of the Port Authority's public relations department and the woman who encouraged the entity to build the world's biggest building. Her idea would eventually become the Twin Towers. I spoke with Joanna about her novel. So I can't do justice and describe the story that you've written. Can you tell me in your own words what your book is about?

Joanna Scott: It begins with a gathering organized by a woman named Lee Jaffe who, in the 1950s and '60s, was a powerhouse female executive who worked for the Port Authority of New York. So in this opening scene she gathers her secretaries—the clerical girls, she calls them—and she is giving them advice about careers for women, hence the title of the novel: *Careers for Women.* She warns the young women about some of the obstacles they will face and then offers herself as a model of success. From there the book dives into both the past and the future of that gathering. I move around in time; I explore the lives of a couple of the young women who worked for Lee Jaffe. The narrator of the book, her name is Maggie Gleason, becomes friends with another young woman who is taken under Lee Jaffe's wing named Pauline Moreau. Maggie discovers that Pauline Moreau has a deep, dark secret. Things get complicated in Pauline's life. Maggie takes charge of her young daughter, and then Pauline disappears. And the book sets out to solve the mystery of Pauline's disappearance. At the same time it is following the business life that is generated by, weirdly, the Port Authority of New York. They were responsible for building the World Trade Towers. And a little interesting footnote about Lee Jaffe—she's an actual historical figure—

she was the one who came up with the idea to build the tallest building in the world to house the World Trade Towers. And so I thought that was an important thing to consider as I explored her life and the lives of the fictional characters around her.

Tschernkowitsch: And I found it so interesting that you chose to make Lee Jaffe one of your characters—as you mentioned, a real-life person. How did you stumble upon her story, and why did you want to include her?

Scott: Well, it's kind of hard to come upon her story. She is pretty much forgotten by history. I had saved a bunch of newspapers from the fall of 2001, surrounding the tragedy of 9/11, and a couple of years ago I just decided to go through this bag of old newspapers, actual copies of the *New York Times* and some other newspapers. I'm not sure exactly what I was searching for; I was trying to remember what it felt like in that fall and looking for smaller stories that came out of those months. And one thing led to another, but I saw a mention of Lee Jaffe, and I became very curious about her. Who was this woman who penned a memo, in some ways changed the course of history by opening up the possibility of this huge, huge building that then became the Twin Towers? So it was almost by accident that I came upon her, but then something about her—there's not much written about her. And so I had to make a fair amount up, to tell you the truth. But her forgotten importance, I think, was the thing that became the motivation for me to explore further and see if I could create a story surrounding her that was fictional.

Tschernkowitsch: Lee Jaffe's story is interesting, too, at a time when we're now just learning about contributions that women may have made in all these men-driven fields that were kind of brushed under the carpet and set aside.

Scott: That's right, that's right. Interestingly, I learned that Virginia Woolf once planned a book, and she called it *Professions for Women*. She wanted to think just about this. She had given a talk to a group of women who were working, and she was thinking about how the identity of women would change once there is gender equality—she said something about how we can't really know what women can do until they have access to every field available, open to human skill. She never wrote that book, *Professions for Women*. So in some ways I wanted to pick up where she left off, if that's possible, if that's allowed.

Tschernkowitsch: You have this mystery that you've set up, and there's also the story about women and the obstacles that they face in life and in careers. And there also seems to be this lesson in greed and how far the mighty can fall. Should we draw a similarity between this fire that you have in Visby and then the destruction of the Twin Towers on 9/11?

Scott: You're not the first one to offer that as a possibility. As an author, I'm always hesitant to solve any equations, you know. I'd like to put the possibilities in the fiction and ask readers to consider without preparing them with conclusions of my own. So I think that's a really interesting possibility. I was thinking a lot about the human urge to build. It's unstoppable. We're going to build. It's a wonderful, glorious thing to want to build. But it also creates problems in the world, and I wanted to explore those problems. So I ended up thinking about how a rural community becomes tied up with the construction of the World Trade Towers. And that rural community in the novel is the St. Lawrence River Valley up near Canada, far north New York state. They have a created, fictional corporation; I call it Alumacore. They produce the aluminum that then goes into the World Trade Towers. So the connection between the rural community, the economics, the people, the personal lives—that's where my attention goes, to the connections between the personal lives of those in the rural community and those in the urban community. I wanted to see how those play out, to follow and really get readers thinking about how important it is to remember these connections that bind us as Americans.

Tschernkowitsch: What do you hope readers take away from your book?

Scott: I think as a writer one of the things I most long for is the experience I seek as a reader when I'm involved, absorbed by the best books. I want to absorb readers, but I want them to come away with a sense of heightened possibility, of imagination that's perhaps lit up a little bit more, a sense of their own creative powers. That's a pretty broad description of what I'm after as a writer, perhaps. It can account for my motivations for any book. For this book in particular, I was thinking a lot about what it meant to be a woman in the fifties and sixties in this country. I was thinking a lot, to be honest, about the pretty significant backlash we're experiencing in this period of our country's life. So I guess I want people to think in particular about the hurt that can be generated by misconceptions regarding gender, problems of inequality. I think I want people to consider, as I was saying earlier, these important connections between different economies, those in an urban community—it's really important to think of where all the materials come from that we use to build these gorgeous, magnificent buildings. So those are a few things, some more general, some more specific, I guess.

Tschernkowitsch: Well, Joanna Scott, author of *Careers for Women*, thank you for taking time out of your day today to talk to us.
Scott: Well, thank you for giving me a chance.

A Roundtable Forum with
Joanna Scott

Michael Lackey, Athena Kildegaard, and
Corinne McCumber / 2018

Institute for Advanced Study (IAS) Roundtable at the University of Minnesota with Joanna Scott, recorded on March 29, 2018. Reprinted by permission.

Athena Kildegaard: I am going to start with a very brief sketch of some of what is up in Joanna's novel *Careers for Women*, which will give everyone a sense of where we are headed. *Careers for Women* is the story of three women: Lee K. Jaffe, or Mrs. J as the girls who work for her call her, is the public relations director of the New York Port Authority. Pauline Moreau, a beautiful and impetuous woman, works as a prostitute when Mrs. J hires her. And Maggie Gleason, the narrator, is a young woman who has come to New York, as she says, "in search of a husband." She also works for Mrs. J. These women's stories unfold synchronously with the construction and destruction of the Twin Towers and of the company that supplies aluminum to the Towers, a company near the Canadian border that is illegally polluting. That should give everyone a sense of what's up in the novel. But I would like to know how this novel got started. Lots of novelists I know get started because they have got a character that is dogging them, and they have to write about it. So what got you started on this novel?

Joanna Scott: I am always on the lookout for the kind of prompt that comes by accident, by coincidence. The more deliberate I am, the more I try to convince myself, "This is a great idea, and it's going to make a great novel, and I'm going to write it," that's the one that falls apart. When it comes to the fiction I write, my intentions never work out according to plan. And so I know from experience to keep my eyes open for unexpected influences. A few years ago, I decided it was time to go clean out our attic, which I hadn't touched for a decade. You can imagine what was up there. Among the forgotten boxes and bags, there was a paper bag full of old newspapers, national and local, that I'd saved, all from the fall of 2001, all about the destruction of the World Trade Towers. So I brought the bag downstairs to my office, and I started to read through the newspapers. Having the hard copies increased the feeling that I was reading about the immediate reaction to the tragedy. In the immediate aftermath of the attack, we were all stunned. Fifteen years later, I could read the reports in a different light and see portions of the story I'd missed.

Some of the articles treated the history of the Towers, and in one paper I came across a brief reference to a woman named Lee Jaffe. She was the head of the publicity department in the fifties and sixties for the Port Authority of New York and New Jersey. The Port Authority was responsible for the planning and building of the World Trade Towers. What I never knew was that the idea for building the World Trade Towers came from Lee Jaffe. The Port Authority's original plan for a trade center was to build a lot of small buildings in Lower Manhattan. Lee Jaffe said, "Nope. If you want a major trade center, you have to make it the tallest building in the world." Her idea was so popular among the Port Authority directors that they doubled her suggestion to build the tallest building in the world, and they built two towers. I thought, "Wow, who was this woman?" I must have missed the reference to Lee Jaffe back when I was first reading the papers in 2001. I started to do a little research about her. There really is not much information about her. You can find basic facts about any of us now on the internet, so I was able to find a few things about Lee Jaffe and her role at the Port Authority. I can say now that it was the lack of information that made it possible for me to approach her as a subject. I know that some writers really need a lot of information about their subject if they are working with a biographical figure. I tend to be just the opposite. The less information I come up with, the freer my imagination is. I did turn up an interview with Lee Jaffe that ran in a newspaper in the 1950s. The quotes from her were so striking—she suddenly became fully vivid to me. With Lee Jaffe, I had a character I could put in a fiction.

But a character is not a novel. I had to build up the fiction around her. She creates a kind of center for the novel, but the main events happen around her, without fully including her. How I got from her to the fictional characters is a bit of a mystery to me. I'm not sure how it happened. One thing I will add is that, at the same time, I was writing an essay about a photographer named Vivian Maier, whose work had been recently discovered in an abandoned storage locker. Maier was a photographer who worked as a nanny and lived very quietly, without fanfare, and never had a single exhibition of her work. She was a street photographer and did her photography mostly in Chicago and in New York City. I was thinking a lot about her while I was just starting to conceive of my novel, and I found in her photographs illustrations for the setting I was imagining—New York in the fifties and sixties. I pay tribute to Maier in the novel—she's the unnamed photographer who is taking pictures in the neighborhood where the towers are about to go up. Somehow, with the help of those photographs, I made the leap and began writing the novel.

I was surprised to find myself writing a novel about a murder. Don't ask me where the plot came from. I don't know. It just happened. And unlike other novels I've written, this novel came to me, like a punch in the face. Once I had the important components that I've described, the whole thing came to me at once. I was starting to conceive of it in the spring of 2016. That May, I had a one-month residency in Marfa, Texas, all by myself. I was given a little house—and a car—and for one month I did not speak to a single soul, except to my family on the phone at the end of the day. And I wrote this book. I sat there in that little house in the middle of the Texas grasslands, and I worked insanely. A spell came over me. When the month was over, I had a draft of the book. And then I looked at what I'd done and thought, "Uh oh." I had to take apart the draft and do a ton of slow, painful work. But it was a glorious way to work.

I imagine a number of you out there are writers, so you know that sometimes writing is a struggle. We begin with a page that is as blank as this white table. And then other times the writing starts to click and move, and this was one experience when it really started to move for me. That makes it difficult to recreate what exactly happened, how the fiction came to me. But at least it gets us started.

Michael Lackey: As you know, Joanna, the biographical novel is a relatively recent development in fiction. What some of you in the audience might not know is that there was a boom in biographical fiction during the 1990s, and Joanna's novel *Arrogance*, which is a brilliant biographical novel about the Austrian artist Egon Schiele, was one of the first novels from that surge in biofiction. Joanna has also written *De Potter's Grand Tour*, which is about her great-grandfather. I'm really interested in these novels where you take an actual historical figure but you convert them into fiction. *Careers for Women* is a really fascinating version of the biographical novel, which is why I'm interested in this Lee K. Jaffe character, who is a real person. Can you specify one thing in her life that inspired you to write this novel? Can you also tell us one thing that you invented about her, some of the stuff you did that's totally fictional? And can you tell us what you were trying to accomplish with that character?

Scott: From the little bit of information I gathered about her time at the Port Authority, Jaffe seemed to be beloved by her staff, but she had high expectations. She came across as a very powerful, strict woman. Yet she is quoted in one interview saying, "I'm just wild about clothes." And I thought, "That doesn't sound like her." But I used it in the book because I thought it shows the sly side of Jaffe's character. She says what her interviewer expects her to say because she is a woman. The actual news article with that quote begins by saying: "You would not expect the head of publicity for the Port Authority to be a slim woman wearing a beret." That's true. Also true is that she had a little dog. I have to admit that I tend to forget what I've invented and what is real by the end of a novel. Certainly Jaffe's musings, her conversations—any conversations that she has with Maggie or with Pauline—are invented. Her role in the novel as Pauline's savior is an invention. Pauline is the girl who arrives in Lee Jaffe's life with absolutely nothing, no home—she is clearly my invention. But I have to tell you, this was the first biographical novel that I've written that drew a response from the character's living relatives.

Kildegaard: No way.

Scott: Yes. I didn't expect it. Jaffe had no children, but I didn't think about the extended family. Well, one day I received an email, and it began, "Dear Joanna Scott, I almost dropped my coffee cup when I read the *New York Times*." She was Jaffe's niece. Bless her, she ended by saying: "Thank you for making my aunt immortal." She was really pleased with the portrait of her aunt. And, weirdly, the character in the book seemed to match the aunt that the niece knew. I don't know how I was able to get Jaffe's character right because I had so little information about her. But the niece said, "That's exactly what I knew of her." And she also added—for those who have read the book, let's see what you make of this—the niece of Lee Jaffe wrote to me to say, "When I was growing up, I was warned: 'You better be careful, or you'll grow up to be just like Aunt Lee.'" Just like Aunt Lee, who was a working woman, unmarried, without children. The niece and I both found this very funny, since Aunt Lee turned out to play a significant role in the recent history of our country. As for biographical characters, I'm thinking that for the next book, I'll go back further in the past.

Lackey: In your biographical novels, you give us a character from history. And yet, you do not give us biographical or even historical truth. Can you specify the kind of truth you give readers in your biographical novels?

Scott: Critics are making a useful distinction between works of fiction that involve biographical characters and works of fiction that we traditionally called historical. And it has been very interesting, from my perspective, to read Michael's work and his interviews with biographical novelists. I've learned that I'm not alone in sharing some deep skepticism in terms of what we used to call the historical novel. There are a lot of writers who draw from history, who name their characters after real figures but say, "I am not writing a historical novel." That has been illuminating to me, and it has made me wonder what it is exactly that we're pulling away from when we reject the label of "historical novel."

Let's consider the changing role of fiction. I have been noticing in our world of so-called fake news that of all things it seems to be fiction that is taking the hit. Even writers who write novels are starting to talk about it more critically as a genre. Fiction is said to be weaker, softer, than nonfiction. And some writers will go to biography to find more concrete subjects. Notice the metaphorical language that writers use—concrete, versus weaker, softer. Biography has concrete information. It is the opposite of weak and soft. It has been argued that if they bring those facts into fiction, they somehow legitimize the form. But I don't think literature, or fiction in particular, needs to be propped up in this way. Imagination does not need to be made legitimate. The creative work that the mind does when it is leaving behind verifiable information won't be saved and made newly legitimate if it is imbued with facts. I get nervous about that effort. More than ever, I want to insist that if we give up respect for the imaginative work that is the foundation of fiction, we do so at great peril. We lose something that has been really important to world culture for a long time. I am worried that we are giving it up. I'm not even sure what role literature plays in our educational system. And given the craziness of social media and the way certain news feeds blur information and propaganda, it's understandable that readers are looking for trustworthy forms. I, too, want to know what's true in the world, in reality.

So why should we bother with fiction? It just gets in the way and takes up room on a shelf. I guess, then, to finally come around to your question. When we are not writing biography, when we are not writing fact, and yet are introducing fact into fiction, is there a benefit to such a confusing mix? I suppose I think of the novel as a kind of theater. All art is theatrical. I get a chill whenever I walk into an empty theater and see that the stage is all set up. I love to see how a set has been designed to suit a specific production. It's all fake. It's all unreal. But I love the unreal. And so it's in the masking, it's in the costumes, it's in the things we construct as alternatives to our world—these made-up things of culture can reveal so much about the way our minds work. Now this is the only time I'm going to boast. Do you know the show *Criminal Minds*? They began with a quote from one of my essays. It was a quote about how masks are wonderfully paradoxical because they conceal, but at the same time masks reveal how we want to be seen. This is what I'm trying to do in my fiction. I design masks that reveal the very truths they are designed to hide.

Corinne McCumber: I have a book-specific question, having to do much more with *Careers for Women*. How did you envision the relationship between Sonia and Robbie Whittaker? And, to provide some background for everyone listening, Sonia is a child who has impaired motor skills and mental abilities, and she is the daughter of Pauline, one of the main female characters in the book. Robbie is the son from a previous marriage to Kay Whittaker and the adopted son of Bob Whittaker. So Robbie is a legitimate child of a previous relationship, whereas Sonia is an illegitimate child and her biological father is Bob. So, with that noted, Sonia's disabilities are the result of birthing complications and possible neglect by doctors. Your narrator states that "Money—or lack thereof—makes nurses inattentive and doctors downright brutal, or so they were in Pauline's case if her fuzzy memory is at all accurate." Her situation is so different from Robbie's situation, and yet they are both parallel in that they are Bob's children. So how did you decide to give Sonia those specific developmental disabilities? And why did you—or, I should say, did that factor at all into your decision to give her more of a happy ending?

Scott: It's interesting that you pulled out the why from that question, because I was just about to say I can't answer the why, but you got there before me. I think you would understand why writers would be reluctant to say, "I did this because . . ." The how, though, is a good subject to explore—

and out of the how you'll probably get a hint about the whys too. There is a personal reason that I wrote the character of Sonia as I did, and that has to do with a project I've been involved in for almost a decade now. I work with adults who have an array of special needs. They gather once a week at the university where I teach and with students create literary works through a process of interviewing and careful editing.

I started this program with a young woman named Latrice, who has cerebral palsy, and I've gotten to know her very well. I'd been working with her and her housemate, Toni, who had Down syndrome, and what I found with my interactions with them is that they have incredible stories to tell and hadn't had the chance to tell them. Toni composed a really expressive autobiographic piece, and Latrice told a short story about a fictional girl with CP, who, at a certain point, gets up out of the wheelchair and uses a motorized walker to walk down the hall. Latrice was telling me the story, and I was writing down her words as she was speaking, and suddenly she stopped the story and said, "I did that too. I once walked." I made sure to keep that line in Latrice's story. It's really an incredible piece, maybe we could call it autofiction since it moves between autobiography and fiction. And Toni's piece was full of such vivid memories. She could speak specifically about a dog that scared her when she was five years old.

After we'd worked together for about a year, we wondered what to do next. Latrice had the idea of involving students. So we created a program at the university, and now we've just finished our eighth year. It's a life-changing experience for many of the people involved. Through this program, people with difficult communication challenges get the chance not just to express powerful feelings, but to shape their personal expression through a process of editing and revision. Maybe this can reflect on the earlier question, what kind of truth do we want to convey? Without question, we find truth when language is generated by a forceful and generous purpose and is carefully arranged.

My work with this program through the years is behind my decision to give Sonia a presence in the novel. Latrice, especially, has made me think about how we actively produce fulfillment in our lives. And my fictional character Sonia—for those of you who haven't read the book, I'll give you a little teaser—Sonia is the one, just because of the reading she does toward the end of the novel, who makes it possible for the central mystery of the book to be solved. So she does play an important role in the book.

Kildegaard: I have an environment question. The writer, novelist, essayist, environmental activist Scott Russell Sanders wrote an essay in the late nineties in which he complained that American novelists were not writing about the wilderness. And he goes on in that essay to say that all fiction is a "drawing of charmed circles." So it seems to me that in your novel there are two charmed circles: one—you guys have clearly heard about here—which is the south half of Manhattan where the World Trade Center is, and the other charmed circle is the Alumacore plant, this aluminum plant which is close to the border of Canada and is on the watershed, and there is some wilderness surrounding it. I feel like Sanders would be happy about your novel. He would be like, "Yay, somebody finally put the wilderness in a novel." So I would like to hear you talk about these two charmed circles as aesthetic but also ethical choices.

Scott: One, I am from western New York, so for those of us who have lived and spent years outside of the metropolitan center of New York, we sometimes feel forgotten by the state. The particular region I focused on in the novel is the St. Lawrence River Valley, and it is beautiful. It spills out of the Adirondacks toward the Thousand Islands. It is an area that is laced with streams, creeks, rivers; the soil is very fertile. The waterways flow into the St. Lawrence, which in turn flows out to the sea. In the mid-twentieth century, a network of dams was built on the St. Lawrence, and that created a great source of power for industries. Power brought new industries and employment up to the region. It also brought intense pollution that is absolutely stunning in its scope. This pollution has caused severe physical problems for some of the inhabitants of that area. But at the same time, the factories offer an abundance of jobs.

When I learned about the aluminum that is produced in the region, I got to thinking: the World Trade Towers didn't come from nothing. They needed materials. Where do you get materials? You get them from the factory, literally. The Twin Towers used a lot of aluminum, and I learned that they were sheathed in aluminum. Some recent theories suggest that aluminum, heated by the fires and then flooded by the sprinkler systems, caused internal explosions in both towers. Anyway, there is in that area of the St. Lawrence River Valley a couple of big aluminum plants. This is one case where I did not use the real name of the company. I didn't want company lawyers emailing me and saying, "Just dropped my coffee cup because I saw you were writing about our aluminum plant." But, of course, it's all fiction. Any resemblance to reality is only a coincidence.

About reality—the pollution from the factories most impacted the Mohawk reservation, the Akwesasne reservation. The farms used to be incredibly fertile—it was a productive agricultural region. The headwinds and waterways carried the pollution onto the territory and destroyed some of the farms. There were stories of a strange white powder falling in the summer months and coating the grass. The cows developed such intense bone disease that they would collapse from their own weight. Their bones would just dissolve, and they would collapse. There is documentation about this. I include some actual quotes in the book from documents that I found in the little public library up in the region. I stopped in the library without knowing what I was looking for, and I just happened to stumble on files that included handwritten letters as well as official reports. I presume that in some cases, there are no copies of these documents, so they are a treasure. But they are just there on the library shelf for public view. They give details about how the pollution impacted that region over a period of twenty or thirty years.

The effort to address the problem was complicated by the fact that those power dams are shared by regulatory agencies between the United States and Canada, and also the state of New York is involved, and Ontario. So it has been difficult trying to get any one government agency involved in a cleanup effort. It was clear for a long time that this pollution was happening—the industries were dumping waste in the rivers, and they weren't using proper filters in their exhaust systems. It was just terrible, devastating to this incredibly beautiful region of the country. The St. Lawrence River Valley used to be considered a kind of paradise where people had all they needed. They had water; they could grow anything; they had the mountains and the ocean within easy reach. The region is a kind of charmed circle in the novel. The other circle is that neighborhood of lower Manhattan where the Towers went up.

One more thing I really want to emphasize is that the effort of building is a great form of human expression. It is an important, defining activity. We need to build—to build ambitiously, and aim for the sky. Although, I don't know, maybe we need to readjust limits. These pencil skyscrapers going up in New York are making me wonder. But in the novel, I try to honor that impulse to build. We need our buildings. We are here in this great, wonderful building. I keep trying to look at how we balance the urge to build, and the need to protect the environment. We need the materials to build these great buildings, but we need to protect the land, as well. And stupid decisions are made that could be easily corrected. We need to consider the far-reaching impact that connects farmers in a rural region with builders in an urban region. I try to expose the connections between those two circles in the novel.

McCumber: Early in the story, you have Pauline describe her musings over some money that she has come into, and she discusses her views of the men on the bills that she is looking at: They are Alexander Hamilton and Andrew Jackson. She wonders "what they would think if they knew they were associated with a girl who had gotten herself knocked up at the age of seventeen." Your narrator also states that Pauline thought "Andrew Jackson would be more likely to disapprove," while Alexander Hamilton, she decided, "would have a more sympathetic response," telling her to "Take it in stride." First of all, what is the symbolic significance of Pauline's relationship to these larger American ideals in this moment? And what is the nature of these ideals you are trying to pit against each other? And, the third part, were you at all inspired by the musical *Hamilton*?

Scott: No! I can't even get a ticket. Oh my god, have you seen it?

McCumber: No, I have not.

Scott: Who has seen it? [Some raise their hands] Get out. Oh, wow. I have to wait for the travelling show. No, I was not thinking about the musical. When did it come out?

McCumber: The musical came out in 2015.

Scott: Oh, well, so maybe I was aware of it. Pauline was a young girl in the late 1950s thinking she has a lot of money when she really doesn't. It's a lot of money to her that she's been given in order to get out of town because she's not supposed to be there now that she is, as she calls it, "knocked up." So she's fancying that she's having a conversation with her money. She thinks she's rich. She weighs Hamilton against Jackson. It's meant as a kind of comic moment, but also I think we realize, "Oh no, Pauline, you are all wrong here." In terms of Hamilton, he did seem generally to be a nicer man than Andrew Jackson.

Audience member [Susannah L. Smith]: Wasn't he illegitimate himself?

McCumber: Yes.

Scott: Ah! His role in creating the treasury seemed, somehow, to make him more important to Pauline. She wouldn't have the money without him. Not that she would know that, but that may be why he comes out ahead. I do remember that I took out those two bills, and I looked at them when I was writing that section. I asked myself, "What would they be thinking?" The scene was prompted by the visual experience of holding the bills, really. Alright, so are there questions from the group out here?

Audience member [Susannah]: In our conversations here at the IAS we've talked about, in academic publishing, that one sometimes ends up in a bit of a tussle with the publisher about the cover art. I love your cover art. And I'm wondering how you came by the cover of your book?

Scott: It was the publisher's idea. I was given veto power, but I liked it. And in fact a bunch of women working at the publisher recreated the image on an Instagram.

Kildegaard: That's neat.

Scott: It's a cover that I feel successfully conveys the spirit of the book. It gives a sense of the time period, to some extent, through the selections of clothes. And clothes are costumes. As soon as we enter the public realm, we are dressing up in some sense—putting on costumes. We are perform- ing. And fiction can really help us understand what that means, and the relationship between the private and the public. So I thought that the cover captured a kind of performance that I was interested in throughout the novel.

Lackey: I have a question about the character Bob Whittaker. He is a really despicable man in many ways. But what's interesting is that he develops a theology to justify what he is doing, and he starts to believe in a certain kind of God who blesses what he does. At a certain point when he's think- ing about God, he looks at his stepson, and he is fearful that he is gay. He says to himself, "I hope he's not a faggot." That's his word, as I wouldn't use that word. This sets the stage for the end of the novel, when Jerry Falwell is mentioned. After the Towers fall, Falwell blames 9/11 in part on gays. And it's his theology that leads him to do this. There are strange parallels all throughout the novel. Alumacore and the World Trade Center, Whittaker and Falwell—these are parallels that I found very striking. And I wonder if you could talk about why you did that? And were they conscious and strategic parallels?

Scott: I think Falwell had to appear at that point. I was exploring fanaticism and certainty and the way they could lead to delusion. And then I actually read a quote from Falwell, which I use in the book. I didn't make it up. I suppose Falwell's speech can be thought to echo Bob Whittaker. I just want to read, if I can, this section, just so you can hear what Falwell said, the part I wouldn't have had the imagination to make up. It's a section where I'm imagining Mrs. J as a ghost figure visiting the ruins of the World Trade site shortly after the attack. In this scene the dead and the living are filing past her, and she's trying to make her way toward what used to be those Towers—her twins, as she used to call them. She thought of them as hers. So she's walking along, and she sees a hairstylist she once knew, and a man who ran a coffee cart in the lobby of the South Tower. "Here and there, ghosts in unsullied business suits march by. The mayor, accompanied by the governor and the president, leads a pack of policemen trailed by reporters and cameramen. Jerry Falwell strides rudely past, pushing the crowd out of his way. To all you pagans and abortionists, Jerry Falwell is shouting, you feminists and gays and lesbians and the American Civil Liberties Union: I point my finger in your face and say, You helped this happen." I just wanted to get that on record. Mrs. J then scoops up a broken brick and throws it at him. She misses, and he survives.

Lackey: In a lot of your novels you have deep problems with people who have absolute certainty about life. But I do wonder, do you see a difference between those people who are absolutely certain in a fanatical sense and those who are religiously certain in a fanatical sense?

Scott: I do.

Lackey: Because bringing down the Towers was a religious thing. And I do wonder, was there this kind of focus on religion for a reason?

Scott: You are right, though, again, the why of it is a little hard to address. The why is all tangled up in the writing. In the novel I have a few characters who take what they know about religion, and they start to make up their own special story about it that suits them. I'm interested in how the mind does that, how we take something like faith and productively or sometimes not productively construe it, remaking it to suit us. Or we take a legend and retell it, or a rumor, and we make it into something that suits us so we can believe it completely. I like thinking about the way we convince ourselves to believe something. In the fiction I write, sometimes belief leads into the dangerously delusional realm where it provokes inappropriate action. A character thinks, "Of course this is true—I know I'm right." Certainty may be based more on convenience or desire than proof, and it can lead to terrible trouble. Bob Whittaker convinces himself that evil is his destiny, and so he allows himself to be evil. There's an imaginative element at work—Bob imagines himself as Judas and makes decisions based on this imaginative experience. It's great that we can imagine, and, by imagining, form a new thought out of old beliefs. But imagination also can be dangerous. There's a good reason why imagination has provoked mixed responses from philosophers. We need imagination for artistic expression. We need it to think in new ways about difficult problems. But imagination is also the vehicle for paranoia and self-deception. It is responsible for both our good dreams and our nightmares. Imagination influences the stories we tell about ourselves and about our place in the world. It influences the way we think about faith. The more we understand its role, the better we will be at finding the truth in the stories we make up.

Audience member [Julie Eckerle]: So I'm thinking about—I'm not sure exactly where this is going, and if it's a question or a comment—but you use the expression about how the lives are all tangled up in there, and that's a phrase I've been thinking about in connection to the novel, that everything is very densely tangled up, right?

Scott: Beware, readers. The story is told in fragments that are out of chronological order. You don't know where you are in a book; you'll get totally confused.

Audience member [Julie]: And that's part of what I'm wondering, that intentionality behind your narrative choices, because on the one hand entanglement makes a lot of sense as a kind of environmental metaphor. That this is an ecosystem, so if something happens here, it ends up affecting somewhere else, whether it's people or environment or the white substance that falls in both places. And so we've got all kinds of entanglement. Were you trying to do that narratively as well in choosing to fragment the narrative, in choosing to mix up time, in shifting perspectives dramatically?

Scott: To some extent, it is the way I think. I think in shifting, unchronological fragments. When I'm not thinking in that form, I'm faking it. Not really. To think at all, we depend on some aspect of narrative. A single sentence is a narrative, with the words arranged in sequence. But I do like to create unusually ordered sequences, and fragments are useful for this. It's the way I wrote *Arrogance*, actually—with a fragmented structure. It's a form that just makes sense to me, I can't help it. I try to use other forms; I often do use other forms, with long chapters. I've never used a form as radically fragmented as in *Careers for Women*, that's true—except in a few of my short stories. In the novel I offer a comment about the associative power of a narrative. I stick in the hint that we don't have to tell a narrative chronologically, we can tell it through association. And it often is the way we make sense of experience. If you've ever talked to a therapist and paid attention to your monologue, you might be surprised at the odd order in which experiences are remembered. It's fascinating to read case histories and to think about the way memories are communicated. We were talking earlier about Milton's *Paradise Lost*, and agreeing that the stories it tells are "so out of order." The narrative moves back and forth through time—it's dizzying, and really difficult to map out. I don't think I'm alone in thinking in a nonlinear fashion. Poets get to do it all the time. So why don't novelists?

Audience member [Julie]: I'm not judging you.

Scott: No, I know you're not. What you're asking is more about the thematic purpose of a fragmented narrative.

Audience member [Julie]: Right, and is it metaphorical in many ways like the connectedness of the—?

Scott: Right. You know, I did think about that as I was writing about those two charmed circles, the wilderness and the urban environment. It is really hard for people to draw the connection between those circles. They don't visibly connect, but they are connected. The blank space on the page is, in a way, designed to emphasize how we don't see the important connections, we presume that regions separated geographically have nothing to do with each other. As long as they have separate zip codes, they are separate.

Audience member [unidentified]: I want to go back to the process, your writing process in that month in the little cabin. So what did you take with you? How far along were you when you were thinking about this theme? You know, just talk a little bit more about that experience.

Scott: Well, they had a fine small library in this house, so that was very helpful. There were a few great dictionaries on the shelf, which was crucial. There were a couple of reference books that, just by happenstance, were there, and proved useful. In terms of what I took, I had a couple of history books about New York and the Port Authority. I remember as I packed that book, I thought to myself, "I am writing a novel about the Port Authority. Yawn. That doesn't sound exciting." But the books I brought were excellent, and also exciting: one, *City in the Sky*, is about the history of the Trade Towers, and the other was *Empire on the Hudson* by Doig, about the Port Authority itself. Those two books gave me some of the historical foundational material. What else did I bring? I had an outline. I knew exactly where the story was heading. And I'd written an introduction, about twenty pages.

McCumber: So was your outline fragmented like the narrative?

Scott: No. It was rationally laid out, with numbers points, one, two, three, four. What else did I pack? I had my running shoes. Every morning I'd go running out into the grasslands. There was one private ranch that gave access to the public. And I would run and run and run across the land until there was no evidence of civilization in view. I felt like I was on Mars. And the javelinas—one day it was just me and the javelinas. Do you know what those javelinas are? Oh my gosh, they did not want me there. I almost didn't survive. A javelina broke from its pack and came after me. It was fast, but luckily I was faster. What else did I bring? A cell phone. I was reading William Trevor's stories. Every night I would read another Trevor story. He is a great writer, similar to Chekov in the quiet intensity and delicate touch of madness in his stories. And there were a few other books there on the shelf—I read one of the volumes from Eduardo Galeano's lyrical *Memory of Fire*—which is narrated, perfectly, in fragments. It was nice to have a library that was different from my own set of books.

Audience member [Susannah]: So what's fomenting inside now?

Scott: Oh, anger and fury about the current state of affairs.

Audience member [Susannah]: Well, and the novel coming out of that is?

Scott: Well, I've been working on some stories related to the state of reading, actually. I recently published "The Knowledge Gallery"—it's a story in which I express my own nervousness about what would happen if we lost reading. Or if we lost—not the ability to read, but if we lost books. If we lost what we keep in libraries. Because we are losing that. Libraries are emptying themselves out, literally. We recently got the strategic plan from our university library, and it criticized what they called the "*Harry Potter* generation's nostalgia for the books." Isn't that awful? Nostalgia for books, and that's because of *Harry Potter*? According to our library's strategic plan, our university is not nostalgic. "We, of course, are past needing to read books. We are sophisticated, so we're going to get rid of all our books and just have open spaces where you bring your laptops." This cavalier attitude toward reading is just driving me insane right now. So I'm writing a bunch of stories about books that have been lost or forgotten or erased or burned—books that we will never be able to read.

Lackey: I would like to ask a follow-up question that places this idea within the context of your development as a writer. Your earlier stories—and here I'm thinking of *The Manikin* and *Arrogance*—are really dense, complicated. They are definitely in a Faulknerian tradition in the sense that Faulkner is really difficult to read. But *Careers for Women* is a quick read.

Scott: It's interesting that you say that.

Lackey: I have noticed that you are moving away from modernist difficulty over the last few years. My impression is that you worry that the modernist project did not work. I get the sense that you would even say, "Hey, look. All of these great writers, like Joyce, maybe they are not working anymore."

Scott: I don't mean that. No. Maybe it's not working because it's our fault. If it's not working, it's our fault, not the fault of those writers. I don't question the merits of their contribution at this point.

Lackey: But it takes a lot of labor to get through a good Faulkner or Joyce novel. You have to be really committed. So here is my question: is it feasible anymore to write difficult fiction for this generation?

Scott: I wonder. I don't know. That's a question for the younger generation. What do you guys think? What do you want to read these days? Do you want something that makes your head ache because it's so dense and difficult? Or do you want something in which you move with a bang, bang, bang, turning the pages so quickly that you move through it in one sitting?

Lackey: Do you see any value in those old texts?

Audience member [Sarah Severson]: I guess for me, if I'm reading something for fun, I'm not going to read Faulkner, but I have read Faulkner before. And I think when you are forced to sit down and read a text that takes a long time to read because you are battling with it, and you come across a lot more themes and meaning if you are actually taking the time to read through it, and when the text forces you to do that, I think you gain a lot more out of it. And just using your novel as an example, because you don't know how it is connected in the beginning, and by the end you are starting to see how all of it connects, and there are so many layers. And because I had to think through the novel over and over again for weeks and weeks, I ended up with so many more ideas in the end, and so many more revelations and themes that I came across. And if it hadn't been a text that forced me to do that, I wouldn't have gotten so much value from it. So I think, yes, texts—I haven't read Joyce personally, but Faulkner, for one, is forcing you to battle his text and focus more on those ideas.

Scott: So somehow in that work that we're doing—I agree that there's a satisfaction in it. Those were the writers, actually, that made me a writer. That's why I write, because I felt I was learning about the handling of language, and who would we be without our ability to communicate through language?

Audience member [Sarah]: And I think it also allows for more reader interpretation. When you're forced to battle with it in all of its different variety, you're coming up with your own ideas and your own conclusions, and it's all on you to have a response to artistic expression. You need to take more of a stance on it, which, as a reader is really valuable.

Scott: It is, it is. We talked briefly before about that difference between that artistic experience, which is what the writer is doing in creating the text, and the aesthetic experience that the reader has, working with the text. Reading is a dynamic thing. Nabokov said two important things that are relevant to this discussion: one, there is no reading, there is only rereading. What we do after we've finished reading something through, when we return to the text and understand how the pieces fit together—this is the far more valuable experience in his mind. And two, at a certain point in *Pale Fire*—in one of the long footnotes, it's as though he lets the whole fiction drop away, and Nabokov comes in at his most tender and says, "What if suddenly, all of us, we lost the ability to read? What if?" And then he goes on, considering what that would mean. That question seems to be important right now. Great things are happening in visual culture. But as long as we depend on language, we need to keep writing and reading. We cannot reduce knowledge to tweets. Even to call them tweets, that's a stupid word. I read an essay suggesting that the new global language is going to be emojis. We won't even need words.

McCumber: I just wanted to point out that I believe there are fairly different kinds of reading that we do. Because I don't go to Twitter for those deep, complex thoughts that would take me weeks and weeks and weeks. And I don't pick up a novel at the airport wanting to have a life-changing experience. When I try to go deep into Faulkner, into Shakespeare, I'm asking different things from the reading that I am doing. So I would hesitate to make these generalizations about, like, "we are losing reading." I think it would be more like different modes of reading.

Scott: It probably has something to do with my failing eyesight. But that's really important. Yes, there are so many different modes of reading, but there's one that we are in danger of losing: sometimes called deep reading, right now, that you were just describing. [gestures to Sarah] I do think that is, to some extent, in peril. The writer William Gass, some of you might know of him; he called himself one of the last of the decrepit modernists. It's his phrase, decrepit modernist. Not a postmodernist, as he was sometimes called by scholars. No, he was a decrepit modernist. Lately, I kind of feel like that too. I'm still trying to unpack what the modernists bequeathed to us. Something amazing happened in that period, and I fear we'll lose our access to it.

Joanna Scott: A Writing Career in Focus

Michael Lackey / 2019

Michael Lackey and Joanna Scott conducted this interview via email over the course of four months from December 2018 until March 2019. Previously unpublished.

Michael Lackey: You have interviewed J. M. Coetzee and Maureen Howard. What many people probably don't know is that preparing for interviews with great and acclaimed writers requires an enormous amount of preparation. Can you talk about how those interviews (both the preparation and the actual interview) have impacted you as a writer?

Joanna Scott: Those are two writers I admire immensely, but what I remember best about the interviews themselves are their differences. John Coetzee was a writer I'd been reading for years but had never met. I prepared for the interview by reading his books and essays and previous interviews. He was said to be reticent and reluctant to speak about his work, but I was excited by the opportunity to interview him. We began our interview through email, and those exchanges were productive. Then I went to interview him in person, with a little pocket tape recorder. I ended up tossing most of the questions I'd prepared after a few were met with impatience, and I improvised and made up new questions. When I got on the plane to head home, I listened to the tape of our interview and discovered that I could barely hear his responses. I was on a little prop plane from New Haven, scrambling to remember what he'd said, filling in words that weren't audible on the recording. You can imagine how stressful that was. But John carefully edited the copy once we had a printed draft, and I made sure he vetted the whole thing, so that gave me confidence in the finished product.

In contrast, by the time I interviewed Maureen Howard (we did two interviews together), she and I were friends, corresponding and sharing work-in-progress. Her intelligence comes across in her books, of course, but

I also know how incredibly insightful she is in person, with unique powers of perception. I look back through our years of correspondence and am awed by the compression evident even in her short emails. She came to favor long forms in her fiction—her last great work is an interwoven tetralogy of novels. But when it came to conversation and day-to-day correspondence, she favored succinct expression. She had a way of packing complex ideas into fragments of sentences in an off-the-cuff fashion that was both witty and enigmatic. Sometimes I'd come away from a conversation with Maureen scratching my head, puzzled, but then, after reflection, I'd get it. I think I ended up taking in more than I would have if she had spelled everything out. She seemed to be aware of her effect, for she'd often punctuate her comments with, "Do you know what I mean?" The challenge for me in the interviews was to give her the opportunity to express her powerful intelligence in the unconstrained style I'd come to know through our friendship. Also, Maureen and I enjoyed complaining to each other about whatever happened to be bothering us that day—the state of the world, the hypocrisies of literary culture, the cruel business of publishing, the posturing of public figures. But our venting didn't really deserve to be immortalized. The problem was that by suppressing the venting, we had to give up some of our spontaneity. The pitfall of interviewing a friend is that you subject yourselves to an unnatural formality, so it's hard not to come off sounding stilted. Or maybe that's the nature of every interview?

ML: I have a question about what I see as a development in your career. You once claimed that you write fiction in response to Faulkner. I totally get that, but mainly about your early fiction. For instance, *Arrogance* and *The Manikin* are novels that are complex and difficult. I love both of these novels, but I would recommend these novels only to those people who are interested in the challenge of wading through difficult and experimental fiction. But there seems to be a shift in your writing, which I date to about the year 2014. If your earlier fiction could be described as a response to Faulkner, I see your later fiction as a response to Kazuo Ishiguro. Here is what I mean. *De Potter's Grand Tour* and *Careers for Women* are relatively easy narratives to read, so I could imagine recommending these novels to people who are merely looking for a captivating story. And yet, as is the case with Ishiguro, there are haunting and even perverse undertones in both of those novels. But you have to read the works closely and carefully in order to detect those unnerving complexities. Am I right to say that you have moved away from the kind of Faulknerian difficulty that is found in your earlier fiction? And, if so, can you explain what led to that change?

JS: If it's true that my own recent books are somehow more accessible, that certainly hasn't translated into a wider audience for them. It could be that what you call *perverse undertones* in my last two novels were represented more explicitly in my earlier books. I've had plenty of readers call my early work strange. I'll never forget one woman who came up to me after I read from *The Closest Possible Union*—"Such a sweet face," she said, "and yet such a strange imagination." Who doesn't have a strange imagination? Yes, in those days I was under the spell of Faulkner, also Poe, and always Dickens. Does their strangeness make them more difficult? Is the strangeness apparent in my early books more submerged in the recent work? Does that make the books easier? I hope I'm not getting stupider. I believe more than ever that if literature is worth studying, it has to have something to teach us. Whatever else we might learn from reading a novel, we learn what happens when words, liberated from the bondage of facts, are used to create and organize meaning. It's my impression that this very particular learning is becoming increasingly undervalued. I've gone on record to air my concerns about changes in literacy, and I've tried to make the case that if imaginative writing is going to survive as a relevant art, it needs to keep testing its limits. When writers push technique to an extreme, the sheer novelty of the style can seem difficult—literature thrives on this challenge. We see proof in modernism, and, more recently, in the work of Bob Coover, D. F. Wallace, Steve Erickson, Maureen Howard. But difficulty on its own is not an absolute virtue. Writing should aim to increase rather than limit comprehension. I always yearn to be understood.

I do try to keep myself open to all kinds of influence, and from one book to another I will change approaches and techniques. At the time I was writing *Careers for Women*, I settled in with the stories of William Trevor. His poised rendering of eccentricity is unmatched. I suspect that his brilliance had something to do with adjustments I made in my own work. Also, out of necessity, on the many long drives I've been making in recent years to visit family members scattered around the East Coast, I have discovered the joy of audio books. I was astonished at how different the experience of *Ulysses* was when I listened to Jim Norton reading it. The book is pure theater. I listened to T. S. Eliot reading *The Waste Land*, over and over. I also listened to potboilers and thrillers and mysteries: Agatha Christie, Stephen King, Dan Brown, John le Carré—I listened and learned.

ML: Throughout your work I detect an anxiety about the tendency to characterize humans as mere products of their biology or their environment. To counter this, you tend to prize mystery, the idiosyncratic, and the perverse. For many, what makes humans something more than mere mechanistic beings is the spiritual or the religious—here I'm thinking about T. S. Eliot and Flannery O'Connor. But I don't really feel a religious impulse in your work. So I feel like you make the same intellectual move as Eliot and O'Connor, but you do so without appealing to the religious. Can you talk about your aesthetic commitment to mystery, the idiosyncratic, and the perverse? And can you address the issue of religion, whether it plays a role in your thinking or aesthetic?

JS: There's so much packed into your question. Let me start with your references to Eliot and O'Connor. Anyone who is serious about writing necessarily absorbs particular influences from a variety of sources, and Eliot and O'Connor were two sources for me, for different reasons. Jim Longenbach, my life mate, is a poet and scholar of poetry and has been thinking and writing about Eliot for decades, so I've been thinking along with him, reading Eliot, and reading Jim on Eliot. And O'Connor was a writer I discovered in my early formative years and did my best to copy. My earliest failed attempts at fiction were filled with variations of O'Connor's images (oh, those eyes of the dying Mrs. Shortley, like blue-painted glass!). But it wasn't just accidental that I was so open to the influence of these two writers. The religious concerns that power their work were always part of the draw—not because I do or don't believe what they believed, but because belief is one of their key subjects. What do people choose to believe, and why, and what's the result? I've always been especially interested in the way belief necessarily becomes a complex attribute of identity and ends up taking a very individualized shape. My attention goes less toward the general beliefs of any particular faith community and more toward the way belief is experienced and animated in the privacy of a person's mind and becomes a driver of emotions. It's the *different* ways of thinking and feeling and being that really fascinate me. I write portraits, and a portraitist has to represent what is distinct to an individual. I get that my characters may seem a little— or a lot—eccentric, but maybe that's because I put the emphasis on qualities that make a person stand out rather than blend in.

But you also mention mystery. I can't be interested in the unique aspects of an individual without wondering what remains hidden—the secrets that are kept hidden from others, along with the propelling forces that remain hidden from our own consciousness. The subject of belief remains key.

What happens when we don't know what we believe? What fuels fanaticism? What happens when a person is forced against her will to believe something, or to renounce a belief? I write in an effort to explore these questions. Could the exploration itself be evidence of a religious impulse in my work? You see, I like questions—that's why I keep throwing some back at you.

ML: It seems like the mind, the way it processes information and experience, is one of the dominant ideas in your work. So while religion plays a role in your work, you are not so much interested in religion per se as you are in exploring the way certain minds function when they are in thrall to a certain religious ideology. This principle seems to apply to many areas of study—science, philosophy, race theory, psychology, etc. In a sense, your work is very interdisciplinary. But do you see any dangers from taking an interdisciplinary approach? Let me specify what I mean. History plays a huge role in your work, and you even talk about the rivalry between history and literature in your interview with Coetzee. But you are also clear that you like to get history wrong, and that you sometimes do so intentionally. Can you briefly talk about both the virtues and the dangers of interdisciplinary work for you as a novelist?

JS: I keep trying to make the case that fiction cannot compete with history when it comes to accuracy. I don't think it's fruitful to bind creative work absolutely to available facts. My intention is not to get history wrong or to be disrespectful, but rather to organize impressions and responses and make something new. I'm reminded of what Edward P. Jones once said when asked about writing his novel *The Known World*. He explained in an interview that once he accumulated enough information about what the world was like in the pre–Civil War South, he could "lie and get away with it." How much constitutes *enough* information depends on the writer, the intention, and the subject, and not on any set formula. The writer needs to persuade the reader to accept the terms of the work, and every work makes use of different strategies. I like to study how visual artists persuade. To offer one example—a student gave me a poster of Picasso's cubist portrait of the art dealer Ambroise Vollard, and it's been hanging on my office wall for years. I don't look at that fractured portrait in order to get an accurate representation of the art dealer. I look at the portrait to see an artist's creative response to Vollard. It wouldn't make sense to criticize the portrait for being inaccurate, or for misrepresenting its subject. The portrait is intentionally inaccurate. At the very least, it expresses the imaginative scope and skill of the artist; and sometimes there's an added, if elusive, benefit when the subject is a real person. Through its re-envisioning, Picasso's portrait of Vollard just might communicate some aspect of the man that's not apparent in a photograph.

There are dangers involved when representation is anything other than accurate—this makes every creative effort potentially dangerous. Any portrait can be offensive if it's uselessly demeaning, or if an author makes false claims about accuracy. I don't think audiences are more inclined to be critical than in the past, though online venues, especially those that favor oversimplification in the form of sentence fragments, have upped the volume of moral scolding for all fields. It's a lot safer to be on the scolding side than it is to be on the creating side. I just hope writers don't stop taking chances and reaching beyond available knowledge. We have to do whatever we can to preserve artistic freedom.

ML: When you say the creating side, what exactly do you mean? Can you give me a specific example from your work to illustrate?
JS: With every opening of every work of fiction I've written, I have to untether myself from information and make a claim that isn't factual. To create something new, I have to imagine, as fully as possible, what it's like to be someone else—a small boy, an adolescent girl, an old man, a snowy owl.

ML: There is a difference between creating a character and creating a new way of thinking or experiencing the world. Reading Virginia Woolf's *Orlando*, for instance, enabled us to see sexual identity in a new way, and only two years after the novel's publication, there was one of the first surgeries in which a man became a woman. In an interview, you say that you "want to absorb readers," that you "want them to come away with a sense of heightened possibility, of imagination that's perhaps lit up a little bit more, a sense of their own creative powers." But there is a difference between inspiring readers to become active creators and you as an author creating a new way of seeing and being that becomes a reality outside the text. Can you talk in specific ways about the creating side of literature at this particular point in time?
JS: This particular point in time definitely needs careful scrutiny, intelligent journalism, corrective criticism, and motivated activists. But I have to resist the notion that literature directly creates "a reality outside the text." I'm skeptical that *Orlando* on its own paved the way for one of the first sex reassignment surgeries. Did Woolf, however, contribute to an evolution in

her culture's perception of gender? That seems more likely. I don't want to underestimate the importance of the *indirect* effect artists can have on cultural change—we know it's important because authoritarian governments try to silence artists. But it remains difficult to connect a work of literature to measurable legislative initiatives. I remember being disappointed to learn in graduate school that Dickens, was not, in fact, responsible for the new child labor laws in mid-nineteenth century England—the laws were already being changed before *Oliver Twist* arrived on the scene. Or think of that apocryphal story about Lincoln telling Harriet Beecher Stowe when he met her that her book "made" the Civil War. Historians have put that one to rest in short order. We can be confident that Dickens and Stowe gave forceful expression to the driving concerns of their time, but it gets difficult when we try to pin their words to specific changes.

When writers are persuasive, they help change attitudes, not laws. Try to compare Shelly's claim that "poets are the unacknowledged legislators of the world" with the actual laws of his day—it's hard to find a direct correlation. I don't want to downplay the potential importance of a work of literature or underestimate a writer's driving political and social concerns. But I want to avoid making claims that don't hold up. I'm reminded of a novelist who spoke on a panel about politics and literature many years ago. He went on at length about how writers speak for "the people." After the panel, this writer went out to the parking lot, and he was mighty upset because the hood ornament had been stolen off his Mercedes. I remember looking at the empty space where the hood ornament had been and thinking that maybe this writer should ask the people before he speaks on their behalf.

If we're really keen on linking literature to action, we might learn a lesson from Goethe's *Sorrows of Young Werther*, which was blamed for driving young people to suicide. Goethe rejected the idea that literature should be transformed into reality. The last thing he wanted was for his readers to go out and shoot themselves. To this day, psychiatrists point to a "Werther effect" when trying to explain copycat suicides, though I think they've long since stopped blaming Goethe for it. The important thing to remember about secular literature is that it locates itself at a distance from reality—that separating space is crucial and must be protected, if only to differentiate secular literature from religious literature. Religious literature commands; secular literature suggests.

ML: I wonder if you can talk about shifts in your thinking about the nature, power, and function of literature. You have been publishing since the late

1980s. By your own admission, you have been influenced by the modernists. But you started publishing when postmodernism and deconstruction were all the rage. By the late nineties, postcolonial theory had come to dominate, and in recent years, there has been a backlash against theory. All these major intellectual developments—did they transform your understanding of literature? Have they made you rethink some of your literary experiments? If so, how?

JS: Such an expansive question deserves a better answer than I can offer. It's really important to acknowledge that intellectual debates, even the ones that might seem the most arcane and impenetrable, can reverberate in the art of the same period. And because I'm passionate about protecting creative expression and intellectual inquiry, I do sometimes get embroiled in those debates. However, theory is not my area of expertise. I'm more comfortable thinking sensorially than abstractly. I'd rather imagine the face of one old woman than come up with an argument about general trends. I don't get much benefit from searching a text for ideas that are inadvertently expressed. I'm more interested in advertent aspects of a text—the expressiveness that results from the writer's observant attention. And I also know from long experience that I benefit from staying open to all influences. I remember way back as a college student, in a single week I would read something by, say, Paul Tillich, Coleridge, Goethe, Erica Jong, and John Updike, plus see a movie by Satjayit Ray, plus go to a Grateful Dead concert, plus talk late into the night with friends—all went into the mix of my efforts as a young writer. I remain committed to staying open and attentive to as wide a variety of influences as possible, which means I'm usually wandering off in another direction while trends and fashions go racing past me.

ML: Do you see yourself, and novelists more generally, as cultural diagnosticians? Let me give you a specific example to clarify what I mean. When Virginia Woolf was writing *Mrs. Dalloway*, she wrote in her diary that she wanted "to criticise the social system, & to show it at work, at its most intense." In that novel, Woolf brilliantly exposes the patriarchal horrors of the medical profession of the time, which she does through her searing portrayals of the characters Dr. Holmes and Sir William Bradshaw, as well as the fanatical Christian mindset of the time, which she does through her vicious portrayal of Miss Kilman, who is appropriately named. What makes that novel so powerful and continually relevant is Woolf's ability as a novelist to expose psychocultural sicknesses with such precision and accuracy. Can you talk about the role of the novelist as cultural diagnostician.

JS: Just to observe is to diagnose. Think of the root of the word—it combines two meanings, to stand apart and to know (or recognize). I agree that novelists, like others working in the arts, benefit from standing apart, observing, and making comparative judgments about what they see. Woolf's Holmes and Bradshaw give satirical expression to paternalistic bias, but they have relatively small roles in that capacious novel. Effective as they are, they lack dimension compared to Septimus and Clarissa. Is it really cultural diagnosis that makes the novel relevant? If so, wouldn't we have to read it primarily as a historical document, since Woolf was criticizing her social system, not ours? Her novel stays relevant because it packs in more meaning than your average work of prose. If you're after a diagnosis of social ills, social criticism is usually a more informative source than fiction (consider the long-standing influence of Marx, as opposed to Marxist novels). Certainly satire offers diagnosis, but I find it more interesting when its scope is personal rather than cultural. Minor satirists have fun representing and ridiculing the social trends of their time. Great satirists, from Swift to Nabokov, give individual expression to personal qualities that don't much change over time, like greed, hate, prejudice, vanity, cowardice. . . . It's a never-ending list, so I'd better stop there.

ML: You say that *Mrs. Dalloway* would be limited were Woolf merely criticizing her social system. But let me use one of your favorite authors to challenge your approach to the novel. In 1957, Faulkner described the character Percy Grimm as "a Nazi Storm Trooper," even though Faulkner acknowledges that he had never "heard of Hitler's Storm Troopers" when he first wrote *Light in August* in the early 1930s. Through intense scrutiny of the social system and brilliant writing about it, Faulkner, like Woolf, was able to diagnose a certain kind of mental sickness that led to serious forms of cultural abuse. While the critique is historical and specific, it is also transcultural and transtemporal, which is to say that we can use the works of Woolf and Faulkner to see how a certain kind of sick thinking functions in other places and times. Grimm, Holmes, Bradshaw—they may be minor characters in the works, but we cannot understand major characters like Christmas, Clarissa, and Septimus without taking these sick and twisted minor characters into account. Ralph Ellison, Toni Morrison, William Styron, Barbara Kingsolver, Alice Walker—these are just a few authors who have brilliantly diagnosed cultural sicknesses and have given us ways of seeing how those illnesses continue to infect contemporary culture. In your work and view, can a specific literary critique of a social system effectively illuminate cultural and political sicknesses in a different time and place?

JS: I want to caution against relying too heavily on metaphors from the medical profession to describe the value of literature. Take it far enough, and writers will start claiming an expertise in epidemiology. That's fine if that's what you've been trained in. The valuable training I received from reading Faulkner, Woolf, Ellison, Morrison, and many other writers was in the art of making meaning with prose. They show how groping inquiry can lead to understanding, and they also dramatize the twists and turns of what you aptly describe as "sick thinking." You offer an excellent formula here, connecting the historical and specific to the transcultural and transtemporal. Absolutely, this connection can be an important goal for all artists. I'm reminded of a line in a story from the Italian writer Giorgio Bassani describing the people of Ferrari as "deranged by the war"—it's a striking way of thinking about a culture's response to war, and it could be said about many cultures. But is it diagnostic? Can we even call it truth? Isn't is more accurate to call it an opinion? It matters immensely that it is spoken by a narrator, a fictional participant in the story who, deservedly, has strong opinions. I love that fiction is full of opinions. Sometimes those opinions are completely unconvincing, often to great satirical effect. Sometimes those opinions are absolutely convincing, giving us the wonderfully satisfying feeling that comes from agreement. Consider the difference between an actual MRI and the artist Justine Cooper's rendering of an MRI—the first is a diagnostic tool, the second is a form of creative, responsive expression. At its best, the opinions of a work of fiction are so forceful, they begin to seem true. But they can only ever *seem*—which is crucial, since a claim that *seems* to be true makes us think a little harder about our own opinions.

ML: One of the great contributions of modernism is the radical questioning of truth. Postmodernism takes this idea one step further by suggesting that all truth is constructed. But is it possible that these intellectual developments have stripped literary writers of their ability to communicate something of meaning and value to the culture? And is it possible that the modernist and postmodernist projects have contributed significantly to the making of Trump and his world of alternative facts? Finally, do you see writers as having any role to play in countering the rise of political movements that are dangerously close to being fascist in nature?

JS: I share the worry that democracies around the world are being threatened, and I shudder with you at the assault on facts. But though we may find fault with the logic of postmodern theory and question its conclusions, we'd be exaggerating its influence to blame it for current political movements.

Fascists are to blame for fascism. Demagogues are to blame for their calculated exploitations.

You're asking about literary writers, though, not theorists. The key word you use is "radical"—this signals that writers are guilty of extremism in the eyes of some critics. Let's consider what happens if we take out that word. We're left with the interesting observations that literary works from the modernist period tend to question truth, and some of the works associated with postmodernism suggest that all truth is constructed. Questioning and suggesting do no more than make their audience think. Questioning and suggesting do not pretend to make unimpeachable claims. I doubt critics mind when a writer suggests that all truth is constructed. It's the radical aspect, the extremism, that's at the heart of the accusation. This tells me that the charge is against the way the suggestion is made, the design, rather than the content itself—the arrangement of language is being faulted for being too radical. To answer that charge, we would need to move carefully through each literary work that counts as radical. Not all radical designs will hold up under scrutiny. We are sure to find that for some books, their volume is turned up too high, they're screechy or disorganized or incoherent. For other books, the design will prove appropriate and sturdy. It's an interesting and necessary investigation, as long as it's carefully conducted. The danger is that critics might be too quick to condemn literary works for generic reasons.

All citizens, including writers, should play a role in resisting corrupt political movements and defending human rights. The few writers who are very visible public figures necessarily have more sway and can weigh in explicitly on policy, most often these days through editorials and tweets, or even, in really rare cases, run for office. In the realm of nonfiction, there is a special kind of power earned from documenting personal suffering as directly and honestly as possible. But let's avoid dictating the scope of literary works themselves. A timely subject does not automatically result in great art. I certainly don't want to go back to a time when critics were accusing women of not being ambitious enough because they didn't write fat books like their male counterparts did. Literature is a responsive art, composed in response to the human condition. We have ample proof that minor subjects can have a major impact. A writer must be allowed to choose whether to focus her sights on something as tiny as a fly banging against a windowpane or as big as a war among angels in heaven.

Index

tales, 35
teaching, 7, 88
technology, 86–87
television, 44, 56, 70
theatricality, 29, 66, 79, 112, 134
Thoma, Geri, viii, 5, 6
"Till the Knowing Ends," xvi
titles, 106
Tolstoy, Leo, 50
Tourmaline, 64–65, 66–67
Trevor, William, 149
Trump, Donald J., 120–21
trust, x, 98, 103, 113
truth, xvi, 46–47, 73–74, 99, 102,
   133–34, 156–57. *See also* authenticity; history

Ulysses, 22, 113, 149

Various Antidotes, ix, 3–4, 9, 50, 64
Vietnam War, 13
violence, xv, 18–19, 25–26, 120
voice, 16–18, 32–33, 51, 73, 79. *See also*
   language

Waiting for the Barbarians, 18–19,
   20–21. *See also* Coetzee, J. M.
Warren, Robert Penn, 96
Waste Land, The, 149
Watt, Ian, 22
White Writing, 21–22. *See also* Coetzee,
   J. M.
wilderness, 135–36
Wood, James, xvii
Woolf, Virginia, xvii, 32, 48, 69, 88,
   97–98, 126–27, 152–53, 154–55
World Trade Center, 121, 125–26,
   139–40
writer's block, 92
"write what you know," 45–46, 62
writing process, 6, 8–9, 74–75, 78, 115;
   changes in, 108–9; for different

literary forms, 63–64; endings, 110;
"false starts," 109–10; habits, 49;
physicality of, 48–49, 91–92, 121–
22, 131; physical location, 121, 131,
142–43; recharging, 88–89; starting,
20–21, 46, 50–51, 72–73, 84, 129–30;
subjects, 118
writing style, 116–17. *See also* literary
   forms; narrative techniques

About the Editor

Distinguished McKnight University Professor Michael Lackey is a scholar of twentieth- and twenty-first-century political, literary, and intellectual history at the University of Minnesota, Morris. He has authored and edited nine books, mostly about the origins and evolution of the genre of biofiction. He has received an NEH Award, the Alexander von Humboldt Fellowship, and a fellowship at the University of Minnesota's Institute for Advanced Study, and he was Martha Daniel Newell Professor at Georgia College in the spring of 2020.

Printed in the United States
By Bookmasters